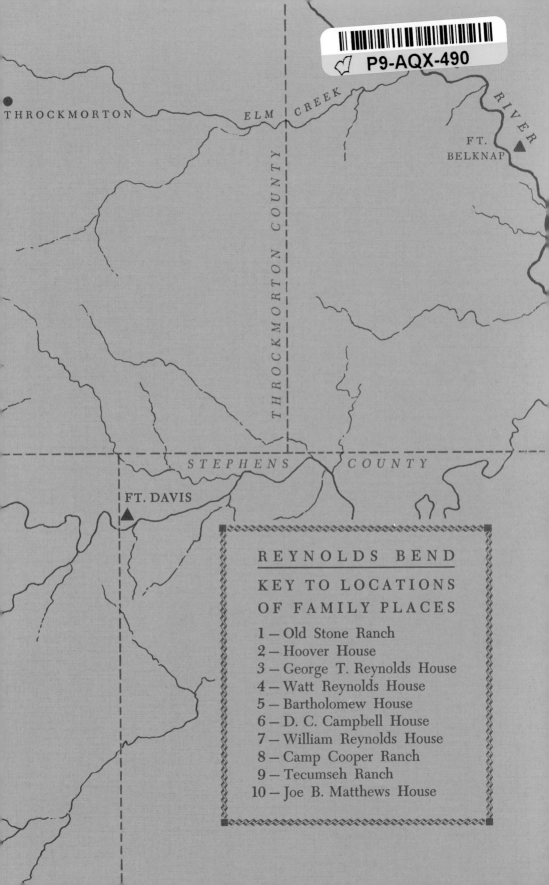

THROCKMORTON

ELM CREEK

RIVER

FT. BELKNAP

THROCKMORTON COUNTY

STEPHENS COUNTY

FT. DAVIS

REYNOLDS BEND

KEY TO LOCATIONS
OF FAMILY PLACES

1 — Old Stone Ranch
2 — Hoover House
3 — George T. Reynolds House
4 — Watt Reynolds House
5 — Bartholomew House
6 — D. C. Campbell House
7 — William Reynolds House
8 — Camp Cooper Ranch
9 — Tecumseh Ranch
10 — Joe B. Matthews House

INTERWOVEN

Number 13

THE M. K. BROWN RANGE LIFE SERIES

JUDGE AND MRS. JOHN A. MATTHEWS

[1880]

INTERWOVEN

A Pioneer Chronicle

BY

SALLIE REYNOLDS MATTHEWS

DRAWINGS BY
E. M. SCHIWETZ

UNIVERSITY OF TEXAS PRESS: AUSTIN & LONDON

International Standard Book Number 0-292-73800-5
Library of Congress Catalog Card Number 73-19485
Copyright 1936 by Sallie Reynolds Matthews
Copyright © 1958 by Watkins Reynolds Matthews
All rights reserved
Printed in the United States of America

Third Edition

Second Printing, 1977

PUBLISHER'S NOTE

Interwoven was first published in 1936 and republished in 1958 in a beautiful limited edition by Carl Hertzog of El Paso.

The University of Texas Press takes pleasure in presenting this third edition, whose design is largely derived from the Hertzog edition, in order to make this fine book available to a wider audience. J. Frank Dobie wrote of it: "Interwoven, more than any other ranch chronicle that I know, reveals the family life of old-time ranches."

We are grateful to Carl Hertzog and to Watkins Reynolds Matthews for making this publication possible.

UNIVERSITY OF TEXAS PRESS

INTRODUCTION

WHEN SHE WROTE *Interwoven,* Sallie Reynolds Matthews's modest intention was a family history for her children and their children. The book, however, became more than a clan chronicle and, from the day of its publication in 1936, found a host of interested readers other than Mrs. Matthews's descendants. It is now well established as a basic source of information for research in the history of the Texas frontier. Long out of print and hard to come by, it is herewith republished by her sons and daughters in an edition befitting its valuable contents.

Mrs. Matthews had perceiving eyes, gentle objectivity and scrupulous regard for the truth. Her story, though written many years after the events of Indian times, is as valid as a contemporary account because she was able to evoke from her good memory accurate recollections. She lay no claim to being a historian, yet, a person of sensitivity, she was often able to convey, as only the best historians can, a clear idea of how it felt to live in the period about which she wrote. When you read her account of the day her family moved into a mysterious, abandoned ranch house on the very edge of the unconquered prairie and see, as her small girl eyes saw, the broken window glass littering the floor, the fang marks left by a wild animal on the door, you sense quite keenly what it must have been like to have been in the family furtherest out from the furtherest outpost.

Though her formal education was limited to spasmodic training under country school teachers, Mrs. Matthews needed no help in writing her memoirs. Having learned her letters from the New Testament, she had bothered all her years, crowded as they were with the rugged demands of ranch life and a large family, to keep her speaking and writing style at a level with that high beginning. This she did not do in pursuit of a program of self-development but because her orderly, eager mind required her to know all that she knew as well and as completely as possible. It was characteristic of her that, besides delighting in the prairie flowers which, at spring time, turned the pastures into a vast, wild garden, she studiously learned their botanical characteristics and names. Her abiding tendency to get things straight makes her book reliable and, moreover, very precious, for to the person with such a tendency the important thing is detail—and *Interwoven* is so filled with the details of pioneer living that it creates much the same impression as a Dutch painting: it is a factual and charming view into the past.

It is also—and not secondarily—a view into the person of an extraordinary woman. She was riding horses when she was a mere slip of a girl. She learned to swim in the muddy red waters of the Clear Fork of the Brazos, instructed by an Indian woman. She went, as a bride, to a distant, lonesome ranch and, in her teens, made a home of a house which was barely more than a shelter. She stood with her husband through every sort of family vicissitude, from the loss of children to the burden of mortgages. Yet rough and trying circumstances never toughened a nature which was intrinsically sweet and full of forbearance. She was not a large woman and in public often appeared shy. Yet everyone who knew her marveled at the unyielding strength, dependable as the sun, which was the essence of her being. She was the daughter of a cattleman and she married a cattleman. Her brothers were cattlemen and her sons became cattlemen. Except for temporary excursions, she lived her life in the isolation of cattle ranches, all located in a relatively small area of Texas. Yet cattle and the cattle industry were by no means her whole life. Her interests were as boundless as the Texas sky above her.

As her grandchildren recall, their almost ritualistic returns to Lambshead, the Matthews headquarters, were infinitely more than summer vacation visits to a ranch—because of her compelling presence. They called her "Other Mama," and that she definitely was—another mother, defining and guiding the first tendencies of their lives. She taught them Bible verses and, greater still, by the example of her own deep faith deepened their own. With her husband she showed them how to work and how to accept the strain of work. And she made it very plain, through her own nobility, that upright behavior, though it is not exactly commonplace, ought to be and, in her family, had to be. All this she did with tenderness and with the result that today, nearly a quarter of a century after her death, her family remembers her with a truly awe-inspiring veneration.

ROBERT NAIL

SALLIE REYNOLDS MATTHEWS

[1938]

FOREWORD

~~~~~~

PERHAPS never before in the history of the world has there been such a rapid and phenomenal development of a country as that of the vast stretch of territory that lies between the Rio Grande and the Bad Lands, a development that took place within the allotted three score years and ten of man's lifetime.

There are some of us yet living who took part in this development, who were reared on the Indian frontier, who grew up with the country and have lived to see it take its place in the sun. We are an integral part of the frontier life of our land, yet we are a part also of this second quarter of the Twentieth Century, this so-called "Machine Age," linking it with the pioneer days.

It is probable, if not certain, that our grandchildren will live to see many new discoveries in the sciences, discoveries as wonderful as the radio, if not more so. But with all the new inventions and innovations that may come in their lifetime, it is doubtful if their mode of living and their surroundings in their old age will greatly differ from that of their youth. At least it is unlikely that there will be the great contrast that there is between our life today and that of our early pioneer days, for it is a far cry from the covered wagon to the high-powered motor car and the fleet passenger plane, from the candle to the incandescent lamp and the neon light, from the open hearth to the electric range, from the signal fires to the radio, and from the Indian frontier to the peaceful ranches where law and order prevail.

Having been urged many times by my children to write my autobiography, I have at last decided to write a sketch of my life for them and my grandchildren. In it I shall endeavor to give as true a picture as I can of frontier life as we lived it.

No doubt there will be some mistakes in this rambling chronicle of two families who have been so closely knit together. Some of the older members of which there are, alas, so few left, may see discrepancies, but I have tried to make what I have written correct in the minutest detail.

There were some tragic and harrowing experiences that have been purposely left out. This family has not been exempt from trials and tribulations. Some seem to have more than their share of grief in this life, and we see others who seem to float along on flowery beds of ease, but we do not know; they may be carrying bitter sorrow deep in their hearts.

I know that I have been blessed far beyond my deserts. I realize there is nothing in me to merit the wonderful blessings I have had. Surely goodness and mercy have followed me all the days of my life and I am truly thankful to the Giver of every good and perfect gift.

SALLIE REYNOLDS MATTHEWS

CHAPTERS

~~~~~~

ILLUSTRATIONS

INTERWOVEN

I   *The Family*

I

I BELIEVE it is customary in writing an autobiography to begin with one's parents or grandparents. Some who are able to trace their lineage from Robert the Bruce or Charlemagne are proud to go back that far. There are no kings or queens among my ancestry of whom I have any knowledge, although it is said that somewhere along the line we all have "prophet, pirate, priest and king" among our forebears. Be that as it may, I am not claiming any of them. There may be a few dukes in the far distant background, entirely too far to shed any glory upon me or my children.

My father, Barber Watkins Reynolds, was of English and Welsh descent, born in Oglethorpe County, Georgia, the son of Benjamin Franklin Reynolds and Sallie Barber. He was a good, honest, upright man, of whom my mother often said, "God never made a more honorable man." While he did not leave his children much of this world's goods, he did leave us the heritage of a good name which "is rather to be chosen than great riches."

My mother, Anne Maria Campbell, was Scotch throughout, descended from the houses of Argyle and Graham, and "rocked in the iron cradle of Presbyterianism" as she expressed it. She was born in Chesterfield District, South Carolina, the daughter of Archibald Campbell and Mary Graham. The literal meaning of the name "Campbell" or "Caimbeul" in Gaelic is "wrymouth" and some of us have inherited that peculiarity to a marked degree.

When my mother was two years old, her father moved his family to Alabama where he became one of the founders of the city of Montgomery and where he owned a large plantation. When my mother was only four years old her father was thrown from a horse and killed, and Grandmother survived him only a month, her death leaving a family of orphan children to be cared for. The eldest, David Calvin, a boy of seventeen or eighteen years of age, took charge of the business affairs of the family. In after years he became probate judge of Montgomery and held the office for thirty-five years. The younger children were separated, being taken over by various aunts and uncles. My mother and her next older brother, Archibald, were taken back to South Carolina and brought up by an uncle, John Campbell. He and his wife spoke the Gaelic together at times when they did not care to have the children or servants know what they were saying, and from them my mother learned to speak the Gaelic as a child.

My mother and father were married in Chambers County, Alabama, January 31, 1841. Six years later, in 1847, they decided to try their fortunes in Texas. Father came out first to look at the country, settled in Shelby County, East Texas, then sent for Mother.

She took a boat at Wetumpka on the Coosa River with her two little boys, George Thomas and William David, aged three and one respectively, and one little slave girl for a nurse. My forefathers on both sides were slave owners. Our housemaid and chauffeur at the present time happen to be descendants of the old family darkies from my grandmother Barber's line.

However, I shall say here that although slaves were rather plentiful in the days of my grandparents, no large number of them fell to my father and mother. This one little girl, who died on coming to womanhood, was all.

From the Coosa River this little emigrating family came into the Alabama River and down that into Mobile Bay, thence to the Mississippi River probably by way of the Mississippi Sound. At New Orleans they took another boat and followed the Mississippi River to the mouth of the Red River up which they sailed to Shreveport, Louisiana, where they disembarked, having been three weeks on the water. It is now an easy two days' trip for a motorist or one of a few hours by airplane.

At Shreveport Mother hired a wagon, team and driver, loaded her trunks, boxes and family on, took her seat beside the driver, and the slow, tedious drive into a strange new country was begun. When night overtook them they stopped at farmhouses along the way.

At that time the name of Texas, more especially West Texas, was a synonym for lawlessness, desperadoes, and all that was wild and bad. It was a haven for lawbreakers from other states who would slip into Texas to evade the law, many of them hiding their identity under assumed names. There were some rough citizens, many of them, no doubt, escaped criminals. But in this conglomerate mass of humanity there was also a leaven of good, those rugged self-disciplined pioneers, men and women of foresight and courage, who were willing to brave the dangerous unknown and undergo countless hardships and privations for the sake of widening their horizons and preparing an easier road for their children and those to come after them. I am proud that my parents and my husband's were of these.

Although feeling very desolate and lonely, so far from kindred and native land, my mother had a courageous spirit and was not

easily daunted when she felt that duty called. My father met
her somewhere on this last lap of the journey and took charge
of his family, to her great relief. Thus began a life of toil and
hardship for one who had been brought up amid the comforts
of life.

The part of Texas in which they settled is a cotton raising
country and in that day and time there was nothing edifying
or elevating on an East Texas cotton farm. So, in 1859, after
twelve years of farm life, they decided to go on west to broader
fields of action where they hoped to better their fortunes and
environment. The children now numbered six, a girl and three
boys having been born in Texas. These were, in order of birth,
Susan Emily, called "Sister," Benjamin Franklin, Glenn and
Phineas Watkins, called "Phin."

When a neighbor man who had been in West Texas learned
that they were going west, he told my mother that it was
"a fine country for men and dogs, but hell for women and
horses," not very encouraging words to one who was about to
go there. The following is an account of the trip and the first
years on the frontier in my mother's own words:

After traveling over a week with slow teams, we landed out of sight
of timber, and the first night's camp on those prairies was horrible to
me, as I had been all my life accustomed, when I awoke in the morning,
to hearing the sound of axes, and the merry songs of the colored race,
but lo, there was no sound to greet my ears but the howling of wolves
and other kindred animals. Oh dear! I was fearfully blue. But all things
have but a time. I kept it to myself and soon got over it. I had fussed and
growled so much about starting, that I would not dare make any complaint.

Ignorance has always been said to be bliss, and so it is. While we were
hunting grass, we were altogether ignorant of finding a country where
the Indians depredated all the time, as they did here — but here we were,
and here we staid. We had a rough introduction to the country, for we
landed in the midst of a big excitement over the killing of a noble young
man by name of Browning, near Crystal Falls.

A small party of men, commanded by Capt. John R. Baylor, went in pursuit. By having some brave and expert riders, they overtook them, and captured a few scalps. When they returned home there was more than one barbecue given them in honor of their bravery. They were very proud of their success, and when the Captain got up to make a speech, he said that he and his men were all hard-shell Baptists, and that "God Almighty went with their sort." Yes, and He goes with those who have not a very hard shell.

Well, the Indians raided on us for a dozen years or more, taking our stock and killing people on the right and on the left. They seemed to be no respecters of persons. If it had not been one of the best countries on the green earth, and guided by a kind Providence, some of us would have been left to starve.

Our children were brought up outside of civilization, as it were. Post office a hundred miles away, a few letters brought to us once or twice a year by chance, no paper mail at all, no preaching, no Sunday School.

The war commenced and we were shut off from all supplies, but the country was covered with all manner of game, and the streams abounded with fish. If we didn't have luxuries, we always had something nice to satisfy hunger. Our boys were all good marksmen, and they killed deer and dressed the skins, and I cut and made coats and pants out of them, and the boys wore them. They were not pretty but they lasted well.

When the war ended I stopped some of that work, I mean my part of it, and renewed our acquaintance with the old familiar taste of coffee. I pronounced it not only good, but very good, after living without it four years.

There were some men in the country who were refugees, out here to keep from being sent to the army. When the Indians made a killing the men always followed, but there were not enough of them to do much good. Those refugees always said they had not lost any Indians and therefore wouldn't hunt for any.

One of my neighbor ladies went out to where the men were mounting their horses, on purpose to tell her husband if they got into a fight, for him to stay behind, but there were so many to hear it, her heart failed. Another woman all out of patience said she did not know what God wanted with so many Indians. It reminded me of a remark an old colored woman made to me in the days of slavery. She said, "That was one wrong thing that God did, when He made Negroes."

Our children were early in life well versed in the hardships and privations of pioneer life, and learned to depend on their own broad views and patient industry.

And now nearly at the close of a busy life, when heart, brain and hands have been filled to the uttermost, we have little to show, yet there may be comfort in the thought that in the midst of innumerable ills that flesh is heir to, we have learned lessons of charity and love, and forbearance. But that doesn't satisfy, the thought comes, shall I go empty handed? I want to carry some sheaves, Heavenly Father, show us the way.

Their first stop in the West was in a little village called Golconda. I have often wondered why it bore that name as it is associated with the diamonds of India and has become a synonym for wealth. Perhaps they hoped to find gold or diamonds near. Later the name was changed to Palo Pinto; it is now the county seat of Palo Pinto County, and yet, no gold or diamonds have been found. The family tarried here for only a short time.

While they lived here, my eldest brother, George, rode the pony express from this place to Weatherford, a distance of thirty-five miles. It was a rather dangerous undertaking for anyone, and seemed especially so for a lad of fifteen years, with hostile Indians roaming at will through the country, picking up every horse on which they could lay their hands. A man on horseback was a target that delighted their eyes; "shoot the man and take the horse" was their creed. My brother was a rather resourceful, intrepid youngster and fared through without mishap in that enterprise.

From Golconda the family moved to Stephens, an adjoining county on the west, then called Buchanan, and destined to become famous for rich oil wells more than half a century later. Here my father embarked in the ranching business. The little place where he located was called the Cantrell Ranch because a man by that name first located it. These ranches usually bore the name of the one who first settled here. The Cantrell Ranch was near the site where the town of Breckenridge now stands.

The county was organized in my father's house. The following are excerpts from an article by B. R. Webb on the early history of Buchanan (Stephens) County which appeared in the Breckenridge *Herald and Commercial* of October 15, 1879:

The first meeting of the County court, as shown by the record, was held Nov. 3, 1860, and it appears therefrom that Gaddis E. Miller was Chief Justice; Geo. James, B. W. Reynolds (my father) and A. Bishop, Commissioners; S. P. Newcomb (later my brother-in-law), County clerk; S. L. Weatherford, Assessor and Collector; James Clark, Treasurer; J. E. DeLong, Surveyor, and T. Matthews (uncle of my husband), Sheriff of Buchanan County. This meeting and the several next succeeding, are stated to have been held at Reynolds' house, which, later in the history, and as civilization and learning began to assert their sway, is designated by the more euphonious appellation of the *Rancho del Reynolds.*

Feb. 18th, S. P. Newcomb was allowed seventy dollars for surveying the town lots, and two dollars per day was allowed to hands employed; but how many hands, or for how many days does not appear.

April 15, 1861, S. P. Newcomb was appointed "to run the unsurveyed boundary lines of the county." Tradition has it that he made the run at the rate of seventeen miles per hour, with a bunch of redskins in full cry after him. That he beat them home is ample proof of the wisdom of the court in his selection for the race.

August 19th, the court met, assessed the county tax at twelve and a half cents on the hundred dollars; allowed the County Treasurer eight per centum for his services; ordered another sale of town lots and adjourned until "court in course."

July 14, 1863, it was "Ordered that an order be issued for the gun-caps and cotton cards that are allotted to this county, now in the city of Austin." These sinews of war not forthcoming promptly, on December 5th following, another order was issued to the Military Board at Austin for the gun-caps and "sixty pair of cotton cards apportioned to this county"; and the county treasurer was allowed $600 with which to pay for them.

May 17th, 1864, it seems that the cards had arrived, and the clerk was ordered to distribute them; Chief Justice Miller was ordered to pay over to the Treasurer the war widows' fund received by him from the Collector, and J. C. Lynch and two others were appointed a committee "to examine into the condition of the widows of the county."

The record also shows that J. B. Matthews, who later became my father-in-law, was one of the first grand jurors appointed.

Here in this little ranch house where the first meeting of the county court was held, I was born, on the Twenty-third of May, 1861, little more than a month after Fort Sumter was fired upon. There were no doctors or nurses to officiate at my birth, only kindly neighbor women who took care of each other at such times. My poor mother thought I was about the greatest calamity that could have happened at that time, a little girl baby coming into this wild, uncivilized country with an internecine war being waged. She thought that she could not possibly live to raise me as she was then forty-five years old. Incidentally, she lived to see my grandchildren. One of the neighbors encouraged my mother by telling her that this little girl would prove God's blessing in her old age. Let us hope she did. I was named Sally Ann for my grandmother Reynolds and my mother. There was no christening for there was no preacher nearer than a hundred miles.

Emerson said, "Happy the man whose home is near a great mountain." There are no great mountains, no great lakes and no great rivers in this land of mine. There are a few big creeks, some of which we designate as rivers, and they become mighty rivers at flood stage, able to float the largest steamer on the Mississippi. It is a land of broad prairies, quiet valleys and vast distances; a land of bright skies, glorious sunsets and most

brilliant starlight; a land where the hills and plains are gay
with lovely wildflowers in the springtime, and where we have
the everlasting hills unto which we may lift up our eyes. It is
a land where the cries of the coyote and the hoot-owl and an
occasional scream of a panther break the nocturnal stillness.
These made the nights seem lonely and desolate to the pioneers
who had been used to hearing the songs of the plantation
darkies until late at night and again on awakening in the
morning.

The life of these early settlers was a nomadic sort, for in those
days no one owned any land. The country was a virgin wilder-
ness with plenty of lush grass, and the rancher moved his herd
at will when he felt the need for fresh pasture. He would select
a spot that looked promising, where he would build a cabin,
tarry for a while, then move on, a good bit like Abraham and
Lot of old, except that they had tents, thus carrying their shelter
with them. Later, when the grass had come again, some other
rancher would come along and occupy the deserted cabin.
There were no permanent homes.

One reason for this was the proximity of the Indians. No one
knew when he might be molested and have to flee for his life.
Another reason was the scarcity of building materials. There
were no sawmills in the country and everything in the lumber
line had to be hauled many miles. There was an abundance of
native stone, however, and a few crude stone houses were being
built. For the most part these pioneer houses were made of posts
set on end in the ground, roofed with smaller poles placed close
together and a layer of soil on top of that. Sometimes there
would be grass and weeds growing on these roofs. The floors
were of flagstones, puncheons or plain dirt.

Furniture was of the crudest homemade sort, chairs of native
woods had seats of woven cowhide strips, bedsteads had the

strips of cowhide instead of the cord of the Eastern states. And yet we sent to California for some "Pioneer" chairs for our present home, as we had kept none of those early furnishings.

II

While we lived at the Cantrell Ranch, our nearest neighbor was a family named Matthews, whose destiny became very closely interwoven with ours as the years went by, so closely that we were almost as one family. The Matthews family consisted of the father and mother, Joseph Beck and Caroline Spears, and four children, Lucinda Elizabeth, called "Bettie," John Alexander, familiarly known as "Bud," Mary and Martha. This was the family when we first knew them. They came to Texas from Louisiana, although Mr. Matthews was originally from Alabama and knew my mother's people there, which made a bond between the two families to start with.

The Reynolds' and Matthews' homes were always centers of hospitality and the wayfarer found a welcome. Of the unattached young men in the country, there were usually several with us, some taking care of small stocks of cattle for themselves. One of them, Flake Barber, a cousin who was caring for his father's cattle, made our house his home for years. In fact, there were always some three or four extra men on the place. I am puzzled now to know how my mother ever managed to cook for, feed and find covers enough for such a family. Nothing ever went to waste; when the men's clothes were cast aside, she washed them and from them made garments for the small boys, and of what she could not use for that, she made bed covers. I realize now that she was an exceptional woman.

And Mother Matthews was another great woman. The Bible speaks of one woman as great, the Shunammite who always had a room, a bed and a candle for God's prophet. Here were two women who, through all the privations incident to frontier life, always had the bed and the candle for God's prophets, although they never had the special room built. I wish to say before going further that I believe there were no two people in this part of the country who did more for the uplift of the community in which they lived, spiritually, morally and socially, than these two women. They "stayed by the stuff" and made the home while the men were at war with the Indians or out battling for a living. It is said, "No country will rise above its homes and no home above its mother." The quiet influence and example of these two homes did much for those who came in contact with them.

Another young man who came to this country and cast his lot with the Reynolds family in those early days was Samuel P. Newcomb, before mentioned as being the first clerk of Stephens County and an early surveyor of the county, a native of Connecticut but late of Missouri. He was an intelligent young man of good education and fine character, an acquisition to the community. He kept a diary, parts of which I shall quote in this account.

About this time my father moved to the Dawson Ranch where we had a much better house, built of logs. It was near a place called Miller Valley, a little settlement of frontiersmen with a number of families near enough together to have a small school. They made Sam Newcomb teacher. The two eldest Matthews children, Bettie and Bud, stayed in our home and attended this school with the Reynolds children. In those early days the pioneer child's school advantages were very meagre.

Soon there came a sad, dark day in the Reynolds family when the eldest son, George, a youth of seventeen, mounted his horse, joined a troop of cavalry and rode away to war. He fought for his country in Arkansas and Missouri, and was home only once on furlough in his eighteen months of service. In the following excerpt from a letter which he wrote home eighteen years later when making a trip to Alabama, he gives an account of his first charge against the enemy.

The day after Christmas we billed ourselves for Memphis, crossing the Arkansas River at Little Rock. The road runs down the valley through beautiful cotton farms, white as the virgin snow with the fleecy staple; hardly a pound of it has been picked, owing to high water. This is a hotbed for breeding "fever 'n 'ager."

White River bottom is rich in water, mud and timber with swamps fifty miles wide. Many places the track sinks deep in the mud making travel slow and dangerous.

We cross White River at Duvals Bluff and soon pass the village of Cotton Plant, the sight of which recalled recollections of my visit to this place eighteen years ago this month. When thinking that President Davis could not possibly run the war business without my assistance, I shouldered my old shot gun and "jined" the army. Here we made our first charge six miles down the turnpike lane. Our command made one stand and at the first fire I shot so hard one hammer of my gun was broken and the other would not work, so I failed to get my man. We had not time to leave the lane, so we continued to charge, and finally made the timber, minus hat, gun, military ardor, and half our force. We started on a scout with fourteen men. We were rash enough to attack Gen. Canby's brigade, then stationed at Helena, Arkansas. The boys who fell into his hands were kindly treated; with the remnant of our scout I escaped into the Mississippi swamps, cold, wet and hungry, and at midnight found an old cotton gin where we hid until morning.

Here I reflected on the probable result of the Davis government and concluded, if it proved a success, it might, but without my valuable services. All my charges on the Yanks after resulted as did the first.

He was discharged and sent home on account of a severe case of measles which was followed by a relapse. After coming home he attended for one winter McKenzie College, a little school at Clarksville, Red River County, one of the older settled counties in the northeast of the state. This ended his school days.

The men who did not go off to war were under frontier service regulations at home. An idea of what constituted such service may be had from an entry in Sam Newcomb's diary, dated January 21, 1865.

Deem it not inappropriate here to say something about the frontier service. The law regulating this service requires us to scout one-fourth of our time, and for the remainder we are permitted to remain at home and attend to our own affairs. Under no circumstances are we to be kept away from home for more than two months at a time, unless actively engaged in fighting or pursuing the Indians.

III

As a natural consequence of a young man and an attractive young girl being closely associated in the same household, a love affair developed which culminated in a wedding. On November 10, 1862, my young sister and Sam Newcomb were married and Bettie Matthews was bridesmaid. This was Bettie's birthday and on this same day a little girl was born into the Matthews family, and was named Susan for my sister whose wedding day it was.

The guests came from far and near as word was passed from one ranch to another. The house and yard were full to overflowing. Preparations had been going on for days beforehand. Improvised tables were placed in the yard and dishes borrowed from the nearer neighbors to accommodate the guests. Piles of cakes, chess pies, egg custards and tea cakes had been baked, turkeys and chickens roasted and beef barbecued. We did not have raisins, currants and other fruits, with the flavoring extracts that we have now, there being only spices for flavor. If one did not have plenty of eggs and butter the neighbors would contribute, and they always helped with the preparations. There was not only dancing but also a candy pull with a big kettle of molasses candy to add to the festivities.

In those early days girls were married very young, too young entirely. There were reasons for this, however, one being the fact that a pioneer life tends to develop boys and girls, maturing them earlier, and another being the high ratio of young men to young women. In a new country there are many unattached young men who come with the spirit of adventure seeking their fortunes, while girls are not so plentiful and therefore are much sought after.

From the Dawson Ranch we moved to the Hanna Ranch where a rather unusual incident happened. One morning the three younger boys were in the dooryard dissecting the tail of a panther that had been killed only a little while before. They were getting the sinews to use in wrapping the feathers on their arrows. Out in front a short distance away, a hobbled horse was grazing. It was customary, when turning horses out, to fasten their front feet together with pieces of cowhide called hobbles, much in the manner of handcuffs. In this way they could graze but could not wander far away. Suddenly two Indians dashed out of a grove of trees on their ponies and began whipping this hobbled horse, making him go as fast as possible until he was out of rifle range. Then they jumped from their ponies and took the hobbles off. While doing this they were joined by several others who had been watching from the cover of the trees.

The young men of the place had ridden out after cattle and had taken all the firearms. There was only one gun left and that was an old one that would not shoot. My father tried to bluff the Indians by pointing it at them. They had a chance there to run in and massacre the whole family, but they only wanted the horse. Bennie recognized some of the horses they were riding as ones that had been stolen before.

In the Fifties there was a chain of forts built along the frontier of West Texas for the protection of the settlers who were pushing their way west. Fort Belknap, Camp Cooper and Fort

Phantom Hill were the ones in our locality. There were many others but these were nearby. It is said that when the soldiers were going out to establish one of the forts, they kept seeing in the distance what appeared to be hills. When they came to the place where the hills should have been, they found they had been deceived by a mirage for there were no hills — thus the name Phantom Hill.

When war came on, all these forts were abandoned, some of the troops remaining in the United States army and others going into the Confederate. Our own Robert E. Lee left this country to join the Army of Virginia. The soldiers were angry from some cause when made to leave Fort Phantom Hill and soon after they had departed, some of them went back and set it on fire. So all that was left of this fort were the stone chimneys and crumbling walls of the few stone buildings. Some of the chimneys are still standing as sentinels after all these long years. There is one little building still intact; it served as either the calaboose or the powder magazine. It has thick stone walls and is covered by a barrel vault of stone. Prickly pear grows from the vaulted roof now, and it is used for a cowshed.

After the forts were abandoned the citizens were left unprotected and the Indians began their depredations with renewed energy. One noted foray was called "the Elm Creek Raid," when they came down early one morning like the Assyrian host, their cohorts gleaming in war paint and feathers rather than purple and gold, with their blood-curling yells striking terror into the hearts of the little band of settlers along Elm Creek, killing men and women, and taking captive other women and children. In after years I became acquainted with some of the people who were carried off in this raid and heard their experiences at first hand.

Fort Davis on the Clear Fork of the Brazos

2 *Fort Davis Days*

THE ELM CREEK RAID so intimidated the ranchmen that many took their families back to more civilized parts of the state. Those who stayed decided to gather their families into closer groups for mutual protection. These groups were called forts. Among them were Fort Hubbard, Fort Clark, Fort Owl Head, where the Matthews family located, and Fort Davis where the Reynolds family cast its lot temporarily. The last named fort was built on the bank of the Clear Fork, a tributary of the Brazos River, this branch being called Clear Fork because the water is sweet while that of the main stream is very strong with salt.

This Fort Davis, which is not to be confused with the old abandoned military post of that name farther west in the Davis Mountains, consisted of some thirty families. A conception of the general plan and construction of the fort is given in an item of Newcomb's diary, dated January 1, 1865.

Fort Davis is on the east bank of the Clear Fork, and about fifteen miles below Camp Cooper. There are now about 125 persons in the fort and others are preparing to move in. There is another fort about twelve miles down the river, but it is not so large as Fort Davis. Fort Davis is 300 x 325 feet, divided into 16 lots, each lot 75 feet square, with a 25-foot alley running through the fort from east to west. This fort commenced on the 20th of October and there are now some twenty good houses here. That is, good

17

houses of the kind. They are built with pickets, covered with dirt, and the cracks are stopped with dirt, and while not very ornamental they are very comfortable.

The houses were set near together and formed a sort of stockade. There was a stone house on one corner, already built by some earlier settler, which was used as a refuge for the women and children when Indians were reported to be near. There were many false alarms, of course, but when a horse would show up some morning with an arrow sticking in him, it was certain that Indians were not far away.

A part of this hastily thrown together group of people was coarse and illiterate with no culture or refinement, but they were not in the majority by any means; they were far outnumbered by sturdy, God fearing men who believed in law and order, and exerted themselves to make Texas a law abiding country, and they succeeded.

A school house was built in one corner of the square and a school was opened by Sam Newcomb. One entry in his diary reads: "Commenced school here today for a term of fourteen weeks. I have only nineteen scholars at present and most of them are rude, wild and wholly unacquainted with school discipline." There was soon a marked improvement in behavior and scholarship, however, as Newcomb was a man of some culture and a strict disciplinarian.

A Sunday school was organized at the home of J. M. Frans. There was no Sunday school literature such as we now have, only the Bible. They would read and discuss a few chapters of that, then old and young would have a spelling lesson from Webster's "Blue Back" Speller, all feeling the need of training along that line.

There was a kind, neighborly spirit of helpfulness at all times in this community. When there was sickness in a family, neighbors helped with the care of the sick one and also with the housework. When there was to be a wedding, they helped with the preparations for the festive occasion. As we had no corner store to which to go when supplies ran low, three or four men would take their teams and drive to Weatherford, a round trip of two hundred miles, and bring back supplies for all. Newcomb mentions one such trip in his diary.

January 31 (1865) — The crowd that left here before Christmas for breadstuff returned this evening. They came in good time as there were not many rations of flour or meal in the fort when they arrived. But people could live here without bread, as there is an abundance of good beef and other meat.

Some rough country lies east of this section and it took this party well over a month to make the round trip.

There was a community milkpen on each side of the fort where the milking was done, mostly by the women. The men sat on the fence with guns to guard against a sudden attack by Indians if there had been a recent report of Indians being near. At one time, some of the men had grown somewhat lax in their sentry duty, as may be seen in the following notation by Newcomb.

March 12 (1865) — Indian excitement has been high here today. About 9 o'clock Mr. McCarty came upon a large body of Indians about three miles from the fort. They gave him a close chase, but he reached the fort all right. The Indians were followed all day but made their escape. I think this will stir some people in this place to do their share of picketing.

All this time the women were carding, spinning and weaving every bit of the cloth for all the clothing worn, making it by hand, as a sewing machine was unheard of in this country at that time. The first sewing machine was brought to this region two or three years after the war by Sam Newcomb as a present to my sister. It was a little thing that was clamped to a table like a meat grinder, and turned by a crank. It made a chain stitch, and the name of it was "Common Sense." How the neighbor women would flock in to sew on that machine!

The reason the cloth had to be made at home was that all the mills were in the North and there was an embargo against the South. It was called a "blockade" then. One of my earliest recollections is of playing around my mother's old-fashioned hand loom and picking up her shuttle when she would drop it.

The women moulded candles and also made all the soap that was used. The soap, as well as soda, was made from lye leached from wood ashes. The ashes were put in a crude sort of hopper made of barrel staves on boards with the ends set together and slanting upward and outward making a troughlike receptacle, wide at the top and narrow at the bottom, which was filled with ashes. Water was poured on this until the ashes were thoroughly wet and began to drip. This carrying water was a slow tedious task which my brothers hated.

A creek not far away was so impregnated with salt that it was no trouble to evaporate the water and obtain plenty of this necessary commodity. Later on it was commercialized by one of the early settlers, Mr. Ledbetter, who processed salt in quantities and sold it, having his own sacks and stenciling.

In those days the river abounded in fish, and game was plentiful. Turkeys, prairie chickens, antelopes, buffaloes and deer were in abundance. That the profusion of wild life particularly impressed a New Englander may be seen in the diary of my brother-in-law.

November 29 (1865) — A large buffalo was driven into the fort this morning, causing a great deal of commotion and excitement. The animal was attacked by forty dogs and killed in a very few minutes.

December 5 (1865) — Cold and sleeting and several herds of buffalo drifted by during the day. I have stood in the school house and watched a herd not more than one hundred yards away. What a show this would be in my native state where there is no wild game larger than a fox; but game of all kinds, even wild hogs and horses, is plentiful here.

My brothers were fond of hunting and had learned to tan the skins of the deer and antelope. From these Mother made suits for the boys, thus saving herself a lot of weaving. The buckskin was soft when tanned, much like the suede of the present time, although the buckskin would stretch and become stiff and hard if wet. That was objectionable as the boys would be caught in a shower sometimes even though rain was not very frequent.

My sister became adept at making gloves from this same buckskin and for these she found ready sale as cowboys like a nice pair of gloves. They would pay as much as three dollars for a pair of gauntlets with fancy stitching, all of which was done by hand, of course. She also learned to weave hair nets from hair taken from the tails of horses, and with the grey, black and brown, she had a variety of colors to match different heads. These nets were quite popular and the young women would spin and weave for her in exchange for a net.

II

As this group of houses was called a fort, the citizens decided they should have a flag, so they asked one of the young women, Myra Sutherlin, to make one. While she was making it, some other young women were busy spinning thread and making the cord with which to raise it. The men planned to make a gala day of that when the flag was to be raised. They invited the citizens from the neighboring forts, Belknap, Owl Head, Hubbard and Clark, to join them in the festivities, and there was much cooking and preparing of food beforehand by the women, for there was to be a barbecue dinner after the flag raising, to be followed by a dance in the evening.

March 2 (1865) — Some time since invitations were sent to all the people in the surrounding country to attend a public dinner on the occasion of the

presentation and hoisting of a flag in Fort Davis. A few ladies and gentlemen from the lower fort and the two Hoovers from Fort Hubbard were the
only visitors present. About 12 o'clock all the soldiers of the fort mustered
under J. G. Irwin, officer of the day, and while the soldiers were in line
and under arms, Miss Almira Sutherlin, followed by a train of ladies and
band music, marched up in front of the line and presented the flag to the
soldiers. I being the person selected to receive the flag from her hand, did
so, thanking her in the name of the people. I then stepped back to the head
of the column and we marched throughout all the streets of the fort in the
following order: First, flag bearer; second, company of soldiers; third, the
band; fourth, company of ladies. After marching through all the streets
we stopped in front of the flagstaff, attached the flag to the flag line and
sent it to the topmast in a trice, midst three loud and long cheers from
Fort Davis. The soldiers then fired three salutes and were dismissed. In
firing the salutes, Mr. Sutherlin got wounded by the cylinder of Mr.
Bryant's gun bursting.

The young folks danced in the school house all night. The school house
being 16 x 30 feet, answers all right for a ball room in size, but not so well
in other respects—the floor being rock, and none too evenly laid.

Thus it was that my brother-in-law recorded the ceremony in
his diary. So the "Stars and Bars" of the Confederacy floated
over this little civilian fort, the pride of all concerned; but the
flag did not wave long, as we were nearing the end of the struggle,
although no one in this part of the country had any idea as to
how long this war would drag on. We were too far away from
activities to know how it was progressing.

In spite of war and dread of Indians, these people seemed to
have a share, at least, of merriment and festivities. There were
always feasting and dancing at weddings. It was no trouble at
all to get up an old-fashioned square dance; fiddlers were rather
plentiful and accommodating. They would play all night for a
small sum. The young men would pass the hat and take a collec-
tion while dancing went merrily on. The women had quilting
parties and were joined by the men when eating time came, and
often the young men would sit around the quilt talking to the

girls. There were candy pulls, the candy being made of molasses in a wash pot out in the yard. There would always be candy making at weddings, which perhaps was for the entertainment of the children principally, although the grown-ups enjoyed candy pulling as well as the youngsters. When nothing else offered itself, there was the age-old diversion of jumping the rope.

On one occasion there was a dance at the home of Mr. Frans, "Uncle Matt," as he was called. Some of the young men had ridden from neighboring ranches, and had tied their horses near the house, which was on the bank of the Clear Fork. When they went out to get their mounts, they had none; they were gone.

In the morning when daylight came, it was discovered there had been another dance under the river bank nearby, for the soft earth had been patted down by moccasined feet. The Indians, too, had enjoyed the music of the fiddlers, and had danced before taking the horses.

One of the pioneer cattlemen, W. B. Slaughter, father of the late C. C. Slaughter of Dallas, was also a missionary Baptist preacher. He came occasionally to our fort and would preach a sermon or perform the marriage ceremony for any young couple who wished to be married. There were people living in this fort who were married and raising a family who had never heard a gospel sermon until preacher Slaughter came to the fort.

One of his visits, I think it was in December, stands out among my childhood memories when Susan Frans and Will Anderson were married and united with the Baptist Church. That meant that they were taken down into the Clear Fork and plunged under the water. What so impressed me was that Will went down into the water wearing an overcoat; it was long and had a cape, the heavy blue coat of the Federal army, evidently brought from the battle front. He must have been a heavy lift out of the water for the preacher. In later years these blue army overcoats were very common and were exceedingly good stuff, as were all of Uncle Sam's furnishings.

Books were not plentiful in those days. As I remember it, the family library consisted of the Bible and Foxe's *Book of Martyrs*. There were a few school books, of course, and there may have been other books, but these two are impressed upon my memory as I learned to read from my mother's large print New Testament at the age of five, and the picture in Foxe's of the old martyr who held his hand over a candle until the back was burned to a crisp to show he was not afraid of the stake, was imprinted on my memory never to be effaced.

III

In May, 1865, news was received at the fort that one of the bloody wars of history had at last come to an end. The poor worn defeated soldiers of the Southern army began to return. I shall say here that no bitterness was instilled in our family as a result of the slaves being freed. I have heard my mother say many times that slavery was a curse to the South and was wrong in every way, that she was glad they were freed, that the North was on the side of right and the right prevailed. But the one thing to which she could never become reconciled was "Sherman's march to the sea." And does it not appear, at this far distant day, a wanton devastation of our fair Southland? That and *Uncle Tom's Cabin* rankled like poisoned darts in the bosoms of many Southerners. There is no doubt but that there were a few Simon Legrees, but those were extreme cases. For the most part the slaves were treated kindly and were well cared for, many showing their devotion to their masters by remaining faithful after they were freed.

After the war closed and the men came home, the temporary civilian forts began to disintegrate. Several families from Fort Davis moved up to the abandoned military post, Camp Cooper, which was situated on the Clear Fork some fifteen miles above Fort Davis, and where there were some substantial houses built by the soldiers and left furnished when they were hastily called away.

In the middle of October of 1865 while we were still in Fort Davis my brother, George, Si Hough and Riley St. John departed with a small herd of beef cattle with the intention of driving them to Mexico, but on reaching Fort Concho they learned that cattle were not selling well there, so they changed their course and headed for New Mexico. On the Plains they met a crowd of men who asked them where they were going, and on being told, the strangers expressed surprise, and said that they admired their "courage but not their judgment." They made it through without any serious Indian trouble or misfortune of any kind, although they did have a number of narrow escapes. They sold their beeves at Santa Fe at a handsome profit, as they were bought very cheaply, cattle being worth little here at that time. My brother had only twenty-five head, which he had bought for eight or ten dollars and which he sold for sixty, thus making a net profit of fifty dollars per head. The expense of marketing the cattle was negligible as they had only pack horses, and their meals consisted of bread and meat. Their meat cost nothing, game being plentiful along the way. Although the expense was small, the danger was great, even though the Indians were not so much on the war path then as they were later.

I have been told that this was the first herd ever driven from our part of Texas all the way through to Santa Fe. At Santa Fe, St. John, who owned an interest in a mine near Pike's Peak, learned that his partners had sold their interest for several thousand dollars, and as my brother and Hough said they could make it back alone, he went on to Denver to receive his share of the mine profits.

George and Si got back to Fort Davis on the 16th of January, 1866, having been gone three months during which time the family received no word from them.

On another trip, Brother George, by an act of kindness, became involved in rather serious trouble brought on by a poor half-witted waif called Jaco whom he had befriended, even to the point of sharing his bed with him. Jaco stole a horse, my brother's horse to be exact, was caught and sentenced by the crowd to be hanged. Death seems a harsh penalty to pay for stealing a horse, but according to the unwritten law of the range, that was the customary punishment inflicted upon horse thieves. My brother pitied the boy and pleaded his case, finally persuading his companions to substitute a whipping for hanging. So, instead of being hanged for stealing the horse, Jaco was flogged. Brother George gave him an overcoat and, if I am not mistaken, a horse, too, and sent him away.

But that did not close the incident. Of all people, it seems that Jaco bore a grudge against my brother, the one who had been kind to him, for he reported the whipping and there was a time when there were men out looking for my brother to punish him for it. If he had let the boy be hanged, nothing would ever have been said, but his deed of mercy brought only trouble. Of course, when the details were brought to light, he was exonerated.

3   *The Stone Ranch*

I

IN THE EARLY part of 1866, my father moved his household which, besides his wife, own children, son-in-law and grandson, consisted of several young men. One of them, Silas Hough, and my brother, George, were as David and Jonathan. The others were Flake Barber, Levi Shaw and Mart Hoover. We had quite a retinue, eight grown men, three young boys ranging in age from fourteen down to eight years, two women, one little girl and a baby boy, for on August 21, 1865, there had been born into my sister's home a little son, Samuel Augustus Newcomb, always called Gus, the first grandchild in the family.

The place where we went had been built by a Captain Newton C. Given who was with the Army and had been stationed at Camp Cooper; it was probably erected as a ranch and hunting lodge combined as he owned a fine pack of hounds. He established this place in 1856 while the fort was being constructed, and he had the advantage of the Government freighters and teams. The shingles, window sashes, doors and such for this ranch house as well as for the fort were hauled from San Antonio, a distance of more than three hundred miles.

The ranch is five miles above Camp Cooper and about twenty miles from Fort Davis. I presume we did not get an early start and had slow teams for we camped one night on the way. I do not remember the camp; what I do remember are the buffaloes that we saw when we were nearing the ranch. They are migratory animals, coming south in the winter and slowly moving north in the spring. The country at that time was open, not covered with mesquite timber as it is now, and one could see a long way. I do not remember the month but it was in the late winter before the buffaloes had gone north, and on that day, hills, plains and valleys were simply covered with them. Every way that one looked and as far as eye could reach, there were the stately animals. They appeared much like a gigantic herd of cattle that had been rounded up in a bunch, then allowed to scatter out, so thick were they. It is little wonder the ranchmen were not sorry when they were exterminated even though it did seem a wanton destruction, for they ate up the grass from the domestic cattle and were a general nuisance to the ranchmen.

II

The Stone Ranch, so called by our family because it was all built of stone, even to the large corrals, lay in an open valley with beautiful hills to the south and, at a farther distance, to the west and northwest. Not far to the northeast there is a little peak which we have always called Buzzard Peak and beneath which flows the Clear Fork whose winding course came to within less than a mile of the ranch house. It was situated in what is now the southwest corner of Throckmorton County and was on the outside border of civilization. The country just northwest of us was occupied solely by Indians and wild animals for hundreds of miles; great herds of buffaloes, deer, antelopes and wild horses roamed the plains. The nearest ranch, Camp Cooper, was five miles east.

It was a bright sunny day when we came to the Stone Ranch,

and although the house was not very large, it appeared to be a veritable fortified castle with its thick stone walls, and seemed a haven of peace and quiet to the family after having lived in the crowded fort.

The house stood on the north side of a little creek we called Walnut because of the many trees of that species which grew along its banks. Across the creek on the south was a spring, covered by a stone house, where we kept milk, butter and meat in the warm weather.

The main building consisted of only two large rooms with a fireplace in each room, and a wide hall between with heavy double doors of oak opening on both north and south. The hall was made into a bedroom by closing one side. One room had a plank floor; the other room and the hall were flagged with stone. On the north was a detached building with two rooms, one with a fireplace. This we called the "bachelors' hall" as it was occupied by the young men and boys.

On entering the house, we found it in a state of disorder. Some of the windows were broken and the glass was lying on the floor. Some wild animal, a wolf or panther, perhaps, had evidently been in the house, as one of the inside doors had been badly gnawed on the edge. The sight of those glaring toothmarks gave me an eerie feeling; I could imagine many and all kinds of wild animals visiting us at night time. How such things impress children! I can see that dusty and glass strewn floor, and that door deeply marked by animal teeth, in my mind's eye now. The work of putting things in order was started at once when Mother began to sweep, and Brother George took the broom from her, saying, "Let me sweep."

There were a few pieces of furniture in the house when we took possession, some chairs and a little French bedroom suite in white, decorated with a spray of flowers on the head and foot boards of the bed and on the dresser drawers. To my childish eyes this furniture appeared about the last word in elegance.

One day Glenn was nosing around in the old rock quarry near-by when he spied a wooden box which on examination proved to be filled with dishes. I think there was almost a full dinner set of ordinary white queen's ware, decorated with tiny roses in relief. I remember there were several covered vegetable dishes. This was a rich find for the family as the supply of china had become so depleted that there was not enough with which to set the table, and tin ware was substituted. With all this new china the table appeared festive indeed.

There were other things found hidden in these rocks, cowbells, staples for ox yokes, and such, for all of which, together with the pieces of furniture, my father paid when the owners came back.

Finding all these articles made the family feel that any pile of rock might contain hidden treasure, so when a small mound of rock was discovered on a hill close by, the men at once proceeded to investigate in order to see what was hidden there. What they found was a tiny coffin. There was no mark of any kind about this mound of rock to indicate that it was a grave. Of course it was immediately replaced as found, and the little mound is still there, but to this day we do not know to whom the child belonged.

The room with the stone floor in the main house was an all purpose room. Mother's bed was in one corner. At the opposite wall stood a long table at which could be seated twelve or fifteen people, and in some way Mother and Sister managed to set it always with a white cloth, clinging tenaciously to the refinements of life.

The cooking was done on the wide fireplace. On winter evenings after the ovens were set aside, the hearth swept and table pushed against the wall, the family gathered around the fire.

THE OLD STONE RANCH,
built by Captain Newton C. Given in 1856, was still on the outside border of civilization when the Barber Watkins Reynolds family moved into it in 1866. (The drawing is a reconstruction, based upon written accounts and examination of the ruins).

Often the boys would be moulding bullets, Mother and Sister sewing, knitting or mending. Many pecans, which had been gathered along the banks of the Clear Fork or Walnut Creek, a short distance away, were cracked and sometimes roasted over the fire. Now and then the cured tongue of a buffalo would be buried in the ashes and roasted; if you have never tasted this special tidbit you have missed something to delight the taste of an epicurean.

Life was never monotonous to me even though there were no other little girls with which to play. I tagged along after my young brothers, Glenn and Phin, as they played. They would make traps and sometimes get a bird, which was always thrilling. They never put them in a cage, but would free them after playing with them a little while.

On the south side of the creek near the spring house, there stood two magnificent elm trees, the interlocking branches of which, like a huge umbrella, made a dense shade. The soil under the elms was moist and alluvial, a contrast to the rocky, arid hillsides.

One day Mother observed Glenn and Phin, very busy with hoe and rake under these trees. She asked them what they meant by all this work; they answered, "We're making a garden."

"Well," Mother replied, "Nothing will grow in that shade."

This was a wet blanket indeed on their spirit of industry. Phin dropped his hoe, saying, "Humph! I'm not going to work in the hot sun." Thus, garden making was over for the time.

Of course, I was too young to realize the seriousness of life, and it seemed a busy, happy time, full of cheerfulness and useful tasks; but as I look back upon it now, I know it was fraught with much anxiety, especially when the boys were out working with the cattle or scouting for Indians. It must have been lonely and rather desolate for my mother and sister with so little contact with other women. There would be an occasional visitor from

Camp Cooper and Sister would sometimes ride down there with the men, but I do not believe my mother ever left the ranch except one time during our stay there. There were neither newspapers nor magazines to keep us in touch with the world, no church or Sunday school near.

I wonder how my parents kept track of the days with no calendars. My mother did lose the day once when she did her Saturday cleaning and scrubbing on Sunday, and took a quiet Sabbath rest on Monday. As a rule there was a peaceful calm on Sunday, different from other days, but not always, for at times that was the hardest day in the week, with a crowd of extra men to cook for. Although women were scarce, men were fairly plentiful.

Besides the regular household of fifteen, there were many transient men coming and going. Sometimes they came hunting buffaloes and other game; they did not have to search far for buffaloes as they were seldom out of sight of the house from October to May. At other times they were scouting for Indians who had taken their horses.

The chief recreation for the young men was the hunt and this they thoroughly enjoyed. One noted one while we were at the Stone Ranch was when they went up the river to a place they called Blackjack Thicket, near Fort Phantom Hill, where they had hoped to find some blacktail deer. The common red and whitetail deer were very plentiful where we lived, but there were no blacktail. I do not remember that they got any deer on this expedition, but they did get a white buffalo which was a very great rarity, this being the first we had ever seen or heard of, and among the many thousands of buffaloes that were killed in this country, I never saw but one other white robe; it was owned by Frank E. Conrad.

Two of my brothers, George and Ben, had a shot at this one, but George being the elder, got the skin. It was given to an Army officer at Fort Griffin after the Fort was established, to be placed in the Smithsonian Institution at Washington. In my visits to the Capital I have searched diligently in that and other museums and can find no trace of its ever having been placed there. It was there at one time as some of the family saw it, and it does seem as if there would be some record of it. The officials of these institutions have been most kind in assisting me in my search for it.

When summer came my father made his yearly trip to Weatherford for supplies. On this trip my sister and her baby, my brother, Ben, and I were along. The reason for Sister's and my going was mainly to visit with our relatives, the Barbers, and to have some pictures made, little tintypes they were. While we were away the ranch was raided by Indians.

One Sunday morning after most of the men had ridden off leaving only two as guards and the two younger boys, Glenn and Phin, twelve and nine years of age respectively, fourteen Indians, Kiowas and Comanches, charged about the house and fired a few times. Glenn used a gun as well as the two men and the Indians soon left, taking with them five hundred head of cattle that they had rounded up and all the horses they could lay hands on. In those days it was customary for the cattlemen to put the young calves in the pen in order to keep the mothers from straying away too far and to get them located and gentle. (At one time we also had fifty young buffalo calves nursing the cows with the other calves.) There were sometimes a hundred or so calves in the pen. The Indians turned out the calves and rounded in as many of the mothers as they could find, but not all, as some of them were bawling in deep distress for days afterwards.

As Indians were not accustomed to seizing cattle, their usual quarry being only horses, some people think these raiders were not Indians, but rather white desperadoes. If they were not Indians, they were artfully disguised in Indian dress, war paint and feathers, and their war whoops were well simulated, for the family felt certain they were Indians.

Father knew nothing of this incursion until when nearing home he heard that the ranch had been raided by Indians. After this he thought surely the family would return to the fort. Not my little Scotch mother; she was made of more heroic metal. When someone asked her if she had not been terribly frightened, she said, "No, but I was all-fired mad."

III

The next event of interest happened in April, 1867. Some horses had been stolen from settlers east of us and a party of men, riding in hot haste to overtake the Indian marauders, came to our ranch where they were joined by my brothers, George and William, and Si Hough. They overtook the Indians at the Double Mountain Fork of the Brazos, a distance of thirty-five or forty miles from the Stone Ranch. They were loitering here, taking their ease and shooting buffaloes, thinking they were out of the danger zone. They were taken by surprise and only one escaped to tell the tale. They were outnumbered, there being ten white men to seven Indians. One of our men, John Anderson, was shot through the arm, receiving a flesh wound, and a minie ball passed through William's sleeve. Brother George was the only one seriously hurt. He was shot with an arrow that entered his body just above the navel. He was wearing a United States Army belt buckle which was about two inches wide by three long. This buckle, we think, may have saved his life, as the arrow hit the edge of the buckle, breaking the force of the shot to some extent or it would doubtless have gone through his body. These arrows had great force when shot from strong Indian bows. He pulled the shaft out, but the head was left in his body, where it stayed fifteen years. At first they thought it possibly might have dropped in the loose sand when the shaft was taken out and have been covered, but that was not the case, as was proven in after years.

When Si came up and saw George lying there, he swore he would have the scalp of the Indian who shot him. He was not long in getting it. This particular Indian was marked by his gay trappings; his war bonnet of eagle feathers and bridle covered with disks of hammered silver proclaimed him a chieftain, they thought. The silver studded bridle was given to Brother by Si Hough and is now treasured by William's sons, Brother George having had none to inherit it.

William and John Anderson rode all night to tell the family what had happened. The night before they came, my father had a dream which so impressed him that he told Mother that one of the boys was wounded, and he was walking the yard in distress and looking for a messenger when the two boys came. This premonition seemed almost psychic.

How to get the wounded boy home was a problem. They tied two horses together, heads and tails, and filled in between with their packs. The packs, called kayaks, were made of cowhide and were on the order of old-fashioned saddlebags, only they were much larger and were used to put across a pack horse for carrying provisions for cow hunts and scouts like this one. These were placed across the horses and filled in with bedding, and the wounded man was laid on this improvised bed. A man on each side led the horses as the slow journey home was begun. You can realize that this mode of travel was anything but comfortable for an injured man; it was almost unbearable, but he endured it until nearing home when he asked to be put upon his horse which had an easy gait. He wanted the family to see him sitting his horse! They, of course, did not know that he was still alive. When the scouting party approached the ranch, the younger boys were on top of the smokehouse watching, and when they counted the full number it was a great relief and joy to those at home.

In the meantime, Sam Newcomb was riding night and day to Weatherford, more than a hundred miles away, for a doctor, only stopping for a bite to eat and a fresh horse at the ranches along the way, and he and Dr. James D. Ray of Weatherford rode day and night on the return trip. When the doctor arrived, he probed the wound a little and that ended his treatment. It was all he could do at that time as he did not have the facilities of modern surgery. Strange to say, the wound healed without infection and soon he was going about as usual. However, he suffered a good deal of pain in his body until the arrow was removed, although no one would have suspected this from the active life he led.

The arrow head either went into the muscles of the back at first, or in some manner gradually worked its way to the back. Years afterward there was a knot pushed out near his spine which he suspected was the arrow head coming to the surface, and he was right about it, for in 1882 he went to Kansas City and had it taken out. The following are excerpts from an account in the *Kansas City Journal* of July 18, 1882.

Yesterday afternoon there was removed from the body of George T. Reynolds, a prominent cattleman of Fort Griffin, Texas, an arrow head, two inches long. Mr. Reynolds had carried this head sixteen years, three months and fifteen days.

On Friday last the gentleman came to this city and registered at the St. James hotel. His coming was for the purpose of having a surgical operation performed.

Then follows an account of the Indian fight which is omitted here.

On his back opposite the place where the arrow entered his body, he could feel its head. At last he decided to have it cut out and came to Kansas City as mentioned. Scales of rust were removed from the arrow head when it was taken from his body. The point was blunt as if it had been eaten off with rust.

This operation was performed by Drs. Lewis and Griffith, in the presence of Dr. Powell of New York. The gentleman was resting easy last evening and feeling much relieved.

There was no anaesthetic used and before going into the operation he exacted a promise from the doctor that he would stop when asked. Two friends went into the operating room with him to see him through. One of them ran out as soon as the doctor started work. The other, "Shanghai" Pierce, a well known cattleman of South Texas, became so excited when he saw the deep incision that he yelled, "Stop, doctor, you are cutting that man to the hollow." At this my brother called a halt. The cut had missed the arrow head, and had gone down by the side of it. Brother raised himself to a sitting posture and bent forward. The steel arrow head slipped out into the incision.

In addition to the bridle with the silver discs, there were many other trophies of this battle with Indians, bows and quivers full of arrows, beads, earrings and bracelets by the dozens; and with shame I confess it, there were several scalps, scalps not taken in wanton cruelty, but as a lesson to the Indians. It seemed that by using their own tactics against them, they were more terrified; at least that is what was claimed by the white men.

IV

Before going further, I want to state my sentiments in regard to the Indians. While the pioneers of this country suffered greatly in many ways, not the least being agony of mind as well as body, I do not think the Indians were by any means altogether to blame. The white people came to America as Christians. Did not the Pilgrim fathers come primarily that they might worship God according to the dictates of their own consciences? And they did treat the Indians kindly in the beginning and had a friendly welcome by Massasoit. But this did not continue for long, and as the settling of the country by white people went on, we know there were many who cheated and exploited the Indians in every way possible, and in some instances treated them with ruthless cruelty.

One such incident came under my parents' knowledge while they lived in Shelby County. During the rush to the gold fields of California, a party of young men left their neighborhood to go there. In the party there was one foolhardy fellow who boasted he would shoot the first Indian he saw. The first Indian he saw happened to be a squaw, sitting on a log nursing her baby, and in cold blood he shot her. Could anything have been more dastardly and heartless? They were immediately surrounded by Indians and the man who did the deed was demanded, and it was obvious that if he were not surrendered, they would kill the whole party. So they gave him up and he was deservedly flayed alive. They were merciful not to have killed the whole company; that is what Mr. White Man would have done under like circumstances.

Another incident of cold-blooded cruelty on the part of white men was witnessed by my husband when a young lad. There had been a band of Indians in the country, and a young man, son of Mr. Browning, a prominent citizen, had been killed. A party of men were out scouting for these Indians, or any Indians, when they came upon a lone redskin who apparently was lost. He may have belonged to the band which had killed young Browning, or he may not, for no one knew. When found, he was roasting a skunk for his dinner. The scouts ordered him to march off and he did so, never turning his head. He was shot in the back, and Browning was given the first shot to appease his thirst for vengeance. The young lad mentioned above was in the party and he thought it a shocking display of cowardice on the part of the white men. He says that if they had given the Indian some food and a "plug" of a pony, they would have acted more like Christians and perhaps have served their country better.

Some time during Civil War days, I do not know just what year it was, there was a band of Indians of the Kickapoo tribe passing through this country going across to New Mexico. They were friendly and did not molest anybody or anything. But they were Indians, and that was enough in the minds of some people. When they came to the locality where the city of San Angelo now stands, they saw a body of men and not wanting any trouble they sent one of their men out with a white flag to parley with these white men. The white men wanted no parley, they wanted to fight. They killed this peace messenger and forced an encounter in which the white men were ingloriously whipped. And the Indians went on their way without being further molested.

Now I do not hold any brief for the Indians nor am I posing as a Helen Hunt Jackson, but I do think that our race has much to answer for. How are we going to reconcile that "Trail of Tears" when the Cherokees, a peaceful tribe, were forced to leave their little homes and farms in western Georgia and North Carolina, because, forsooth, the white man wanted the land, therefore the Indian must move on. They were sent into the new country of Oklahoma that the Government had provided, and it is a fine country, a rich and beautiful land. But these people did not want to give up their homes where they had spent their lives among familiar surroundings and which they loved perhaps as we love ours. Many of them were old and feeble, and so many died on the way. It is spoken of by those tribes as the "Trail of Tears" to this day.

I think that if they had been treated more humanely from the beginning, there would have been much less rapine and bloodshed. What could we expect of a people that were gradually being driven from their home and country, their hunting grounds being taken without remuneration? When the United States Government did set aside certain portions for their exclusive use, did not the white man try in every way to get a share of that? If by no other means, he would take unto himself an Indian wife, and in that way acquire land. If there had been more William Penns, this would have been a more peaceful country in pioneer days. I, for one, believe a good bit in the inherent nobility of the Red Man.

v

Winter came again and with it the buffaloes by hundreds and by thousands. The country was alive with them. They crowded in so closely about the ranch that dozens were killed so near that Mother, accompanied by one of the boys with a gun, would take her scissors and go cut the long forelock from the buffaloes heads. She cut enough of the forelocks, or mops as we called them, to make a mattress, and a nice soft one it was. I fell heir to this mattress, and in late years have made it into soft pillows and cradle beds. My two younger daughters, Mrs. Brittingham and Mrs. Judd, have the tiny beds.

There were so many buffaloes killed that only the choicest cuts of the meat were saved, usually the tongue and the hump; that was a tenderloin strip between shoulders. There would be hundreds of cured tongues hanging in our smokehouse during the winter. At one time I think we had a thousand.

This year Brother George took another small herd of cattle to New Mexico. Si Hough and others went with him, for usually the cattlemen would put their little bunches of cattle together in one herd when going to market. My brother sold his cattle for a good profit. This time he brought Mother a very handsome broche shawl from Santa Fe.

One day a message came to my mother from a friend, Mrs. Selman in old Fort Davis, saying that she was very ill and wished to see Mother once more before she died. So Mother, though not very used to the saddle, mounted a horse and with Si Hough and Brother George as armed escorts, started out on the twenty mile horseback ride. After they had gone a short distance, Brother said, "Mother, that horse has an easy gallop if you can stick on." They struck a gallop and kept it up most of the way, which was rather a hard ride for a woman past fifty. However, I think she felt repaid when her dying friend held her hand and whispered a fervent "God bless you."

VI

A short time before the close of the war, the Matthews family had moved to Golconda, or Palo Pinto as it was later called, and there, on May 17, 1865, another little girl was born. She was named Ella. From Golconda, they moved to a little village called Pickettville in Stephens County, and were living there while we were at the Stone Ranch, so we were no longer near the Matthews family.

Nevertheless, one member of the Reynolds family managed to keep in rather close touch with them, and on July 15, 1867, there was an event that united the two families, the marriage of George Reynolds and Bettie Matthews. Several of our family went down for the wedding, which was in the evening, lighted by the soft glow of candles, and with a most bountiful spread, dancing and general festivities.

Mother did not go to the wedding but stayed at home to make ready the reception of the little bride. In this she was helped by a friend and former neighbor from old Fort Davis, Mrs. Frans. There was much roasting and baking. This party was called an infare in that day and time, and was held at the home of the groom as a rule. The wedding party came in on the afternoon of the third day, having spent the night at the Stockton Ranch on the way. They were all on horseback and came riding in by twos, with the Newcombs leading, the bride and groom next, followed by some six or eight other couples. There were three fiddlers in the party, one having been hired to play for the dance. He became tired around twelve o'clock and quit the job and went to bed, but another took his place and they danced on until break of day, with plenty of coffee and cake to keep them going, the coffee being made in a sizable wash pot and kept hot over the coals in the fireplace.

The next day all the guests, except the brother of the bride who spent some time with us, returned to their several homes. I am sure they must have been exceedingly tired after the dancing and horseback rides, though young women were quite used to the saddle in those days, that being the most convenient way they had of going about. They rode sidesaddles exclusively. A woman thought nothing of taking a small child behind her saddle and another in her lap, and riding several miles to visit a neighbor. I have done it many times in my early married life.

VII

One day during this summer there was a ripple of excitement in the family when across the valley to the south there appeared a body of men. Everyone was hastily gathered into the house, and guns were looked to as the men made ready for defense against what was apparently a large band of Indians. Soon, however, they could see bayonets glistening in the sun, and as they came nearer the blue coats and brass buttons of a detachment of United States soldiers looked beautiful indeed to this border family at old Stone Ranch. They were most welcome; they seemed as a breeze from another world. They proved to be a part of the Sixth Cavalry that had been sent out by the Government to establish another fort for the protection of this part of the Texas frontier.

4 *Fort Griffin*

I

THE SITE SELECTED for the fort was a hill near the Clear Fork River, commanding a good view of the surrounding country in all directions. This was very different from old Camp Cooper, eight miles up the river, which had been built in a narrow valley with a bluff rising on one side and the Clear Fork bending around the three remaining sides. There was no distant outlook there, and Indians could easily have surprised Camp Cooper, but not this new fort.

Soon all was hustle and bustle. Teamsters came from San Antonio, about three hundred miles south, with doors, shingles, window sashes, hardware and other building supplies. A sawmill was built to utilize such native timber as could be used. There was some post oak and on the river and creeks there was elm and cottonwood timber. This was called "rawhide" lumber, because, I suppose, the timber was green and the planks would warp badly when exposed to sun and wind. The mill was on a little creek near by, which ever since has been called "Mill Creek." The Army had good workmen and they made comfortable houses out of this "rawhide" lumber. As I remember it, they were lined with a heavy canvas which held a thin coat of plaster.

Thus Fort Griffin, named for Captain Charles Griffin, came into existence. The scattered ranchmen began to move in near

43

for the benefit of the protection and for school advantages. Soon there was a string of houses along the Clear Fork, reaching for a mile or more above the fort. Contracts were let for beef, hay and wood, thus giving employment to many. The hay was cut from the native grass on the prairies; they were lush meadows with no trees or shrubs, as now, to interfere with mower. Beef was bought from the cattlemen, so money was put into circulation where it had been about as scarce as the proverbial "hens' teeth." At one time Father Matthews had the beef contract and sold meat at $2.75 per hundred pounds net off the block.

We were introduced to canned goods, tomatoes, fruits, oysters, milk (Borden's Eagle Brand), also sperm candles. We knew nothing of vitamins in those days, our principal food being plain meat and bread, with an occasional sack of dried apples or peaches brought from Parker County. Of vegetables there were none, except the wild dandelion and polk salad in the spring. In the earlier days no one planted gardens; rain was so uncertain it was considered useless. The only wild fruits were plums and mulberries of a very good quality which served for pies in season. Of course there were eggs, milk and butter. At Christmas time the officers would pay as much as three dollars a dozen for eggs with which to make eggnog.

I wonder now how we kept such good health and grew into as strong men and women as we have, with a dearth of the kind of food that is considered absolutely necessary now. We were seldom ailing in any way. My mother was very ill once but that is the only serious illness that I recall in our family. It is true that on one of our trips to Parker County, Phin and I developed a case of "chills and fever." No one knew then that mosquitoes caused malaria; we thought we had eaten too many watermelons and half ripe peaches, and for a long time I did not like either watermelon or peaches. Mother made a tea from a plant, a wild Canterbury bell, called "balmony" by the pioneers. The tea was boiled down with sugar to a thick syrup and fed to us. It was a rather bitter dose, but we took it with a very good grace for the sake of the sugar. We recovered from our chills in course of time, whether from the remedy or the healthy climate and vitality of growing youth, I am not able to say.

The first lemonade I ever tasted came in cans. This was a can of sour sugar that had been wet with the juice of the lemon or citric acid, I suppose, and in this can was a tiny vial of lemon extract. The sugar and extract were stirred into a pitcher of water and we had what we considered a tasty, refreshing drink.

In the fall of 1867 father built a house near the upper end of this line of settlers and moved his family from the Stone Ranch. My brother-in-law, Sam Newcomb, built his home a mile or so west on Collins Creek which comes into the Clear Fork near the fort. He entered into the mercantile business in the little village that formed on the flat just below the fort and which was called "The Flat." This was a very quiet little place the first few years but later became a thriving town that did a large volume of business for several years. It had the usual complement of saloons, dance halls and adventurous women. One noted saloon bore the name "Beehive." On the front was painted a large beehive with this verse in box car letters beneath it:

> *In this hive we are all alive,*
>   *Good whiskey makes us funny,*
> *And if you are dry*
> *Step in and try*
>   *The flavor of our honey.*

While this was a wild frontier town with shooting scrapes common, and was about as bad as a town can be, there have been some things charged to it that were not true. One was the beating to death of an Indian squaw by a white man.

II

Among the people who came to this fort for protection against the Comanches and Kiowas was a small tribe of friendly Indians, the Tonkawas. They were a kindly, inoffensive people, never molesting anybody or taking anything that did not belong to them. They did beautiful bead work and were very painstaking with any handiwork they undertook. Their sewing on the buckskin moccasins and bootees was exceptionally neat. They wore few clothes. The women's dress consisted of a piece of cloth pinned tightly around the waist, coming below the knees, and added to that was a garment of one width of calico with a slit through which they slipped the head. This extended below the waist in front and trailed to the ground in the back and when the wind blew, which was much of the time, it floated out behind like a sail. The squaws were partial to materials with large figures in bright colors. Red and yellow calico we called "Indian calico" because of their predilection for those colors.

These Indians were rather socially inclined; they liked to come into our homes and visit. One day a squaw came to our house with her papoose swung in a blanket on her back, she holding the ends over her shoulders, that being the usual way of carrying their babies. She dropped the little boy on his feet to the floor. He had on a new hat and a pair of red top boots with brass toes, and that was all; from hat to boot tops he was perfectly nude. They were not often that way, however, for as a rule the children had on a little garment of some kind, usually a shirt.

A Tonkawa came to father one day with a story that was most amusing to himself. It seems he had been out hunting one day, when riding over a hill he saw down in the valley at quite a distance some Indians of his own tribe, skinning a buffalo they had just killed. In order to frighten them, he emitted some blood curdling yells, typical of Indians on the warpath. They took him to be a Comanche, and, to use his own words, "they lunned, and they lunned, and they lunned," so this wily fellow went down and helped himself to the buffalo. He told the story with great gusto and could hardly talk for laughing, now and then bending double with laughter. He seemed to think my father would appreciate the account, and it was indeed amusing to him as the Indian acted out his tale.

III

Our nearest neighbor when we lived at this place was the Bragg family, the head of which was known as Uncle Billy Bragg. They were one of the families that lost everything when the Indians made the raid on the Elm Creek settlement. I heard Mrs. Bragg tell the story of this raid. They lived too far away to get to the house into which the women and children had been gathered, and were cut off by the Indians, so they ran down into the creek and hid themselves under a shelving rock that formed a sort of cave. Under the rock went Mrs. Bragg, her two children, a boy of ten and a girl of twelve, and the family dog. Mr. Bragg was away, having gone to Weatherford for supplies. Mrs. Bragg said she was terribly afraid the dog would bark and betray their place of refuge to the Indians, but he seemed to sense the danger and lay quietly. They were under the rock all day, with the Indians some of the time walking over their hiding place so close that they could hear the tinkle of their moccasins. The Indians would wind very narrow strips of tin around the fringe of their moccasins and these made a tinkling noise as they walked.

After a long day the Indians finally left, and when dark came, this little family crept out and went to their home, to find it completely sacked, not a rag of anything left. They had emptied the feather beds and pillows and had taken the ticks. One thing the Indians had overlooked was a lot of raw wool tied up in a blanket and lying on some boards that were placed across the joists; her spinning wheel, cards and loom were left as they had no use for those. The surprising thing is that they did not burn the houses. Mrs. Bragg's eldest son was away in the service of his country, and she had just finished a suit of clothes for him that she was going to send to him by a man who was at home on furlough. She said she hated more to lose the suit than anything else. She told the man, kinsman he was, that if he could get his furlough extended so she might have ten days she would have another suit of clothes ready to send. Out of the raw wool that the Indians had not found, this woman spun the yarn, washed and dyed it, wove the cloth, and in the ten days had the suit ready, even to the knitted socks. It would hurry most of us to take the ready-made cloth and make a suit by hand in ten days. She worked night and day, at intervals taking a nap on this same wool in front of the fire. The family took turns sleeping on the wool. I think neighbors whose homes were not pillaged shared some bedding with them, but I heard her say that she slept on the wool.

IV

Another incident of the Elm Creek raid was told my mother by a Mrs. Clifton, and as usual, I had both ears open, listening with breathless interest to these harrowing experiences. Mrs. Clifton was taken captive with two little granddaughters, Lottie and Millie Durgan, aged four years and eighteen months, respectively. Their mother and an infant were killed. There was a negro woman with two children taken at the same time, and it was her husband, Britt Johnson, who was instrumental in the returning of the captives. He was away from home the day the raid was made, having gone to Weatherford with Mr. Bragg. They came in the next day and he immediately set out in pursuit. After trailing them from camp to camp for many weeks, he finally came up with them, and began at once negotiations for the return of the women and children. As to how these negotiations were carried on and how consummated, I am not able to say. One story has it that the Indians finally agreed to return Mrs. Clifton, Lottie Durgan, and the negro woman and children for a number of horses. Horses were probably the most tempting ransom that could have been offered. It was discovered years afterward that the baby, Millie, had been adopted by Aperian Crow, a chief, and his wife, A-mah-ti, who had no children and they had refused to give her up. I am sure Britt, the husband, had aid from the Government in his efforts for the return of these captives, for Mrs. Clifton, in telling the narrative, said, "Mrs. Reynolds, when I saw the white soldiers, I thought they must be beings from another world, their white faces and blue uniforms looked so beautiful."

But their ultimate return, after two long years in Indian camps, was due to the faithful, courageous persistence of this untutored negro who was not willing to give up his wife and children without a desperate struggle. I went to school with Lottie, a rosy-faced, black-eyed girl, pretty in spite of a mark that had been put on her forehead by the Indians, a tattooed ring the size of a dime or a little larger.

After sixty-six years had passed away, a woman named Sain-toh-ood-ie, wife of a Kiowa chief, Goombi, was identified as the long lost Millie Durgan. She was discovered at the unveiling of a monument to Quanah Parker near Lawton, Oklahoma, and by some chain of incidents, her identity was established to the satisfaction of her relatives. There had been efforts made in the past for her return but she had been reported dead by the Indians.

V

Here in Fort Griffin I attended my first school, which was taught by a quartermaster sergeant who must have had a love for children or for teaching as he taught his first session without tuition charge. This was before the days of public schools in this country. He opened his school in one end of the commissary, a long building in the fort used for storing corn, flour, etc. He even went to the trouble of tacking several layers of clean white sacks on the seats and backs of the crude benches which he may have made with his own hands, for aught I know. He was a tall, handsome man with light colored hair which he always parted from the front down the back of his head to the nape of his neck.

He invariably opened school in the morning with songs and a prayer. There is a song, "I think when I read that sweet story of old," that I never hear without my mind going back to that schoolroom and teacher Stackhouse. He was very nice to me,

Picket House built near Fort Griffin in 1872 by W. H. Ledbetter. The houses constructed at Fort Davis were similar but had flat dirt roofs.

often taking me behind him on his big, fine horse and carrying me home after school. This, of course, I loved; what six-year-old would not? But alas and alack! after teaching this school two sessions he disappeared betweens suns, and with him went twenty-five thousand dollars of Government money. He was a fallen idol of my childhood. He sent this saucy message back by some means, "A swift team, a good buggy with wheels well greased; catch me if you can." He was never caught, and if anything was ever heard of him from that day to this, I do not know it. No doubt he changed his name and lived in security and comfort ever after.

In going to the school we passed through the parade ground usually at the time the soldiers were on dress parade in the morning, and it was an inspiring sight to see the soldiers in their blue uniforms with every brass button shining like gold as they stepped along in perfect unison to the music of the military band. We became familiar with all the bugle calls and to this good day I thrill to the sound of a bugle note.

The establishing of the fort brought many worth-while things to the citizens, not the least being the social contacts. The first commandant was General S. D. Sturgis, Lieutenant Colonel, Sixth Cavalry, Brevet Brigadier General. If he had a family I do not remember it for he was there only a short time. When he left, young Captain Adna Romanza Chaffee, destined to become in later years lieutenant general and chief of staff of the United States Army, was put in command of Fort Griffin. It was while he held this post that he distinguished himself in a fight with Indians on Paint Creek.

Mother and Sister were soon on very friendly terms with Mrs. Chaffee and Mrs. Kendall, the wife of a young lieutenant. I think the officers' wives must have been glad to have someone extend the friendly hand of welcome, as they were strangers in a strange land and no doubt lonely and homesick for kindred and friends. As a rule the pioneer women shunned these newcomers; some, besides being greatly prejudiced against Northern soldiers, were doubtless rather afraid that they would be snubbed. It was a sort of inferiority complex, I suppose. There was none of that about my mother; she thoroughly enjoyed the company of these young women and mothered them in a way. It was a red letter day in the life of this pioneer child when we were asked in to dinner (which then was the midday meal) with Mrs. Chaffee or Mrs. Kendall.

There came a day when lovely Mrs. Kendall died, and the pitiful part was the fact that the young husband was away on a scout and did not get home until after she was gone. I think her death was rather sudden from some unsuccessful operation.

The only real sickness my mother ever had in my lifetime was at this place when she lay ill for weeks with typhoid dysentery and Dr. McEldry, post surgeon, a sweet and kindly man, took care of her.

The officers and their wives often rode horseback and frequently came out our way. One time they had a guest visiting them, a young lady from Baltimore, whom they took on one of these rides. She fell or was thrown from her horse near our home and they brought her into our house. She was bruised up a bit, but her chief lament was that she had ruined her silk stockings, and could not get any more nearer than Baltimore. Well, I had never heard of silk stockings in those days, for all I had ever seen of any kind were hand knit of cotton or wool. As for Baltimore, that place sounded much farther away than Egypt does now, and in point of time it was as far or farther. I think it took three weeks to make the trip.

VI

In the early summer of 1868, we made a trip to Weatherford, but not for provisions this time as we could get them from the sutler's store in the fort. The family went particularly for a visit, I think. My father had a double first cousin, Samuel Barber, father of the aforementioned Flake Barber, who lived near Weatherford, and we always visited his family on these trips. Father's business was to get cow ponies. Si Hough and Rice Derett went along on horseback to drive the new horses back. Sam Newcomb accompanied us to get a load of drygoods for his store, and Sister and Gus were in the party.

After spending a few days visiting we started for home, and as we left in the afternoon, we did not get very far from town that day. It was almost sundown when we stopped at a spring on the side of Kee-chie Mountain, a few miles out, where we intended to camp for the night. After seeing the print of moccasined feet in the mud around the spring, that plan was changed; the shadows of evening were falling and the place had a sort of lonely look as I recall it now. We drove on until it was dark thinking we might elude the Indians, then made a cheerless camp without fire or supper. Father, Mother and I slept under one wagon, the Newcombs were under the other, and the two men and Phin were off a little way among the mesquites.

Sometime in the night Si was awakened by the tinkle of Indian moccasins as they passed near his head. When he looked up, he could see a lariat swinging over the head of a horse. He very quickly roused the camp, and the Indians ran away, but they had caught all the gentle work horses except one. Sam Newcomb had had four horses, for one pair of which he had paid five hundred dollars a short time before in Missouri; this was a heavy loss to him.

Before leaving Weatherford, we had gotten some watermelons which we did not have then in our locality. When Phin was aroused, in all the excitement he said, "Well, if the Indians are going to get us, we might as well eat a watermelon."

The next morning there was nothing to be done but to hitch these raw cow horses to the wagons. There was much rearing and plunging and they started off at a gallop with that loaded wagon. This did not last long, they soon quieted with the load they were dragging. The one gentle horse that was left was hitched by the side of an unbroken one to the wagon the family rode in, but we did not choose to ride for awhile; all started out walking until the horses calmed down a bit. The double team would balk at every hill and refuse to pull. The men would get at each wheel and push while one pulled at the horses' heads, and in that way they would get the wagon up the hill. The horses went along very well on level ground, and we made it in without further mishap.

VII

The summer of 1868 saw the first break in our family circle, beginning with the departure of Brother Will who decided to try his wings on a new venture by taking the little herd of cattle that he had accumulated, and driving them to the western markets.

In those days it was customary for men to join in making up these trail herds; often a number of men would throw their cattle together making one large herd and in that case they would share expenses. As a rule, however, there would be one man who owned the main herd; he would furnish the outfit and pay expenses, but would allow men with small bunches of cattle to join him, as they would furnish their own horses and help with all details, in other words, make a full hand. Sometimes the men with the small herds would be paid wages by the main outfit;

such arrangements depended entirely upon the individual in charge.

Brother Will put his little bunch in with Charles Goodnight, an up-and-coming man of the country, and started for Colorado. Goodnight was associated with Mr. Oliver Loving, a prominent ranchman who was taking his cattle to market.

After getting over into New Mexico, Mr. Loving for some reason decided to leave his outfit and ride on ahead to Fort Sumner, taking with him Billy Wilson, a young man with only one arm. They were attacked by Indians on the Pecos River, after reaching a point some distance from the herd. Loving was wounded and their horses were taken, but they managed to escape the Indians and hide themselves under the river bank where they stayed two or three days. Mr. Loving, being too badly wounded to walk, urged Wilson to go and try to get help, as they both would perish if they stayed here. Wilson started back on foot to meet the herd, but being weak from hunger, he did not go many miles before he gave up and lay down in the shade of a Spanish dagger near the cattle trail. Here his brother, Fayette, who was with the cattle, found him ready to die from hunger and thirst. In the meantime, the herd had gone on beyond the place where Loving was.

After being somewhat restored, Wilson guided a rescue party to Mr. Loving's hiding place under the banks of the Pecos. They found him almost dead from hunger added to weakness from his wound. Loving was picked up and carried by some Mexican teamsters to Fort Sumner where there was a garrison at that time, and was put in the hospital, but he did not live long; his privations and exposure had been too great for a wounded man.

Meanwhile, the combined herds, which were two or three weeks in advance, had pushed on and reached Colorado. Brother Will sold his cattle and started for home. When he arrived in

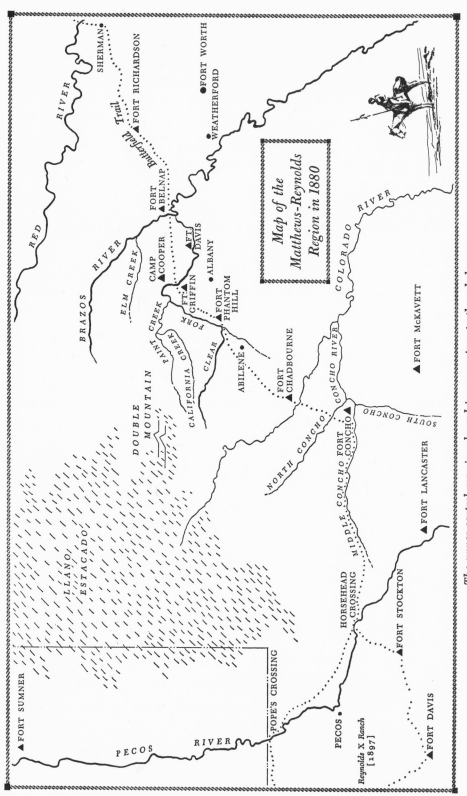

Map of the
Matthews-Reynolds
Region in 1880

RED RIVER

SHERMAN

FORT RICHARDSON

Butterfield Trail

●FORT WORTH

●WEATHERFORD

BRAZOS RIVER

ELM CREEK

FORT BELNAP

CAMP COOPER

FT. DAVIS

FT. GRIFFIN

●ALBANY

FORT PHANTOM HILL

PAINT CREEK

CALIFORNIA CREEK

CLEAR FORK

ABILENE ●

COLORADO RIVER

FORT CHADBOURNE

DOUBLE MOUNTAIN

FORT McKAVETT

NORTH CONCHO

CONCHO RIVER

FORT CONCHO

SOUTH CONCHO

LLANO ESTACADO

FORT LANCASTER

MIDDLE CONCHO RIVER

HORSEHEAD CROSSING

POPE'S CROSSING

FORT STOCKTON

▲FORT SUMNER

PECOS RIVER

PECOS ●

Reynolds X Ranch
[1897]

▲FORT DAVIS

The upper central area is enlarged in comparison to the whole map.

Fort Sumner and found that Mr. Loving had died, he and Loving's son, Jim, and young Bud Willet set out for Weatherford with the body in a wagon, one driving the wagon and the other two as guards and out-riders. It was a dangerous undertaking, not one of the three brave youths being much over twenty years old, but it was successfully carried to completion.

In this same year of 1868, my oldest brother, George, decided to go West and began to get together an outfit, wagons, oxen, men and horses. He had been working and trading since he was a mere youth, and with some help from his father had accumulated seven or eight hundred cattle of his own. Added to these was his wife's dowry of two hundred nice young cattle that her father had given her, which made a fair sized herd.

There were many preparations to be made. An Army ambulance was bought and fitted up with a bed and other things for Sister Bettie's comfort. I remember that she and Sister sewed pockets on the inside of the curtains for her toilet articles and other small belongings. These old-fashioned ambulances were heavy, cumbersome vehicles with three seats, used for transportation of officers and their families; the two back seats were removed from this one to make room for the bed. Sister Bettie drove the ambulance team most of the time on the trip.

A younger brother, Bennie, who was not very strong at the time, was advised by the post surgeon, Dr. McEldry, to leave school and make this trip across the plains to Colorado with his brother. So he added his little bunch of twelve cattle to the herd and joined the outfit. My father also put in a few cattle and went along.

Another member of this party was a young man named Mc-Lean who had married a cousin of ours, a daughter of Uncle Sam Barber. He was a victim of tuberculosis and was taking this trip in the vain hope of regaining his health. In that time it seemed to be the general opinion of people, doctors included, that the drive across the plains into Colorado was the only remedy for this malady, and there were some who appeared to be benefited, but theirs were cases in the incipient state. Now we would think it almost suicidal for a tubercular patient to follow a herd of cattle through dust and heat across the plains with all the hardships to be encountered on such a trip.

On the morning of the 9th of July, 1868, all was ready for the start. The first stop was to be the old Stone Ranch where they were to spend a few days. Glenn, Phin and I bade them good-bye and left for school, school still being in session even though it was July. When we left home in the morning the place was alive and bustling with men, horses and wagons, everyone stirring, getting ready for the departure.

I did not realize the seriousness of this undertaking, of course, but when we came home in the afternoon it fell upon me like a pall. The place was as silent as the grave, with Mother sitting in the house alone. If I should live to be a hundred years old, I could never forget the desolation that flowed over me in that hour. I went in and fell on my mother's lap and cried my heart out. When one thinks of it, five going out of a family at one time was quite a break. My sister, of course, had moved into a home of her own, but that was near. These were going far away, very far at that time. They were going through a region fraught with danger, danger not only from Indians but other marauders. They had to cross the great *Llano Estacado* or Staked Plains where water was scarce and sometimes there would be much suffering for want of it, especially among cattle and horses.

Water for drinking and cooking was hauled in barrels fastened on a shelf made on the side of the wagon bed, and each wagon carried a barrel. No one dared start across the plains without such a supply of water and at that, they often suffered from thirst.

There was no wood to be had; the cooking had to be done for the most part with dry buffalo chips. I think they must burn very much like the peat used in some countries. It is dried grass that has been massed, and burns very well. They managed to cook with it, anyway. Now and then they would find a few mesquite roots in the ground, left from timber that doubtless had been burned in years past.

Following the trail by Fort Concho to Horsehead Crossing, they reached the Pecos River without encountering any Indians. They did not cross the river at Horsehead Crossing where most trail herds were put over, but for some reason continued on up the river and went into camp on this side.

Some time in the night, Indians dashed in and drove off six horses before the night herders could arouse the camp and get into action, and that was quickly done, too. They told it on Brother George that he jumped up and got into his pants hind part in front, and that Bennie could not find his gun, so calmly went back to bed as he thought it useless to follow Indians without a gun with which to defend himself.

The men gave chase to try to get back the horses, while my father, Sister Bettie and the invalid, McLean, sat crouched under a wagon out of the bright moonlight and waited in great anxiety and suspense, knowing that if the men came up with the Indians, there would be fighting and someone likely to be killed, or they might run into an ambuscade and none get back. But these thoughts each kept to himself. After what seemed an age, they came back without the horses, not having been able to catch up with the Indians which, no doubt, was fortunate, as there might have been lost lives added to lost horses.

The next day all kept a sharp outlook for Indians. Brother George always carried a small telescope and used it often. He rode up on a hill to reconnoiter and in a canyon some distance away discovered a band of Indians which he estimated at a hundred and fifty, so they made all the speed they could that day. When night came, no one thought of sleep, but all stayed up and kept watch. The little wife begged her husband's promise to shoot her if he saw she would fall captive to the Indians.

The following day they pushed on to Fort Sumner where they felt safe from attack by Indians. As all were so tired and worn from loss of sleep and dread of Indians, they decided to leave the cattle without night watchers, and after seeing them settled for the night, all lay down for a much needed rest and slept the sleep of utter fatigue. Imagine their consternation when they awoke in the morning to find the cattle gone, not a single cow to be seen. The men were very quickly in the saddle and on the trail of the lost herd which they soon came up with; the cattle had simply wandered away in search of grass.

When they came to Bosque Grande, New Mexico, now called Roswell, my father sold his cattle and turned his face toward home, joining two other men who were coming to Texas. These men were strangers to my father and he did not feel very safe in strange company for he had quite a large sum of money with him. He had not only his own money which he had received from the sale of his cattle, but also money which other parties had entrusted to his care. In those days payments were not made in bank checks, but in cash, oftentimes gold. The money which my father had was in greenback bills which he carried in a canvas belt worn under his clothing. I can still remember watching him peel those bills apart after the trip.

Back in New Mexico, the cattle outfit went into camp for the winter near Red River Station. Brother George and Sister Bettie boarded at this place, a "stage stand" where the stage drivers and passengers were accommodated. They met with friends from

Texas, Tom Stockton and his wife, Etta Cuington, who had come over the trail the year before and had established themselves here, taking their meals at the same place. They had a pleasant winter with these friends. It seems a very fortunate circumstance that they should have met with them and have had their company this first winter in a new country. They would have been much lonelier without them, and I am sure the Stocktons were glad to have them, as they had gone through a very sad experience on the way.

Si Hough, who had gone out with them the year before and had afterwards returned to Texas to take the trail again, was riding along beside the wagon that Mrs. Stockton was in. While charging his pistol, it accidentally went off and shot Mrs. Stockton's baby in her arms, killing it. This was a terrible tragedy and almost crazed the young man for a time. They had to stop and bury the baby as that was all they could do. There was absolutely nothing out of which to make even a crude box; they could only wrap the little body in a quilt and commit it to the ground. How desolate and heart-breaking that was for the mother and father, only those who have had the same experience can ever know.

These old cattle trails are marked by many graves. Some of them have crude headstones, but not many, as most of them were obliterated as much as possible to keep them from being desecrated. The old Butterfield stage route passes through our ranch, the route which so many wagon trains took during the famous gold rush to California; it has its share of graves.

After the winter at Red River Station, our folks went into Colorado where they sojourned at a place called "Hole-in-the-Rock," and then took the cattle on to California, selling them at an extremely good profit. They spent some time in San Francisco, Sacramento and Salt Lake City before returning to Texas.

VIII

As time went on, Flake Barber decided to take for a wife, pretty brown-eyed Nancy Frans. At this time, there were not yet preachers in our part of the country, so he went to Weatherford to get a preacher to perform the ceremony, bringing back a Primitive or "Hardshell" Baptist, he being the only kind willing to brave the dangers of the trip. The wedding ceremony was performed and Rev. Clark, after preaching a few times to the neglected people, returned to his home. For several months afterward, he would come back once a month and preach for us, always walking the hundred miles because he felt that there was less danger on foot than with a horse to tempt the Indians.

On one of these trips he spent the night at a ranch where some mischievous cowboys thought they would frighten him. The next morning they dressed themselves to simulate Indians and rode on ahead where they appeared on a hill in sight of him. When he saw them, he knelt down, and with his Bible beckoned them to come to him. This put the cowboys to shame and they quietly stole away.

One Sunday night we all went to church as usual when the preacher came, my father taking the family in a wagon. The Newcombs, who lived a mile west of the Flat, had walked down, bringing their little son, Gus, and after church Mother took the sleepy boy home with her. As Sister and Brother Sam were quietly walking home in the moonlight, they saw coming toward them ten Indians riding one behind another, their customary style. My sister and her husband were on the open prairie, not a tree or a bush to hide them, and strange to say, they were entirely unarmed, something very unusual as a man seldom thought of stepping out without one or two pistols swung to a belt around his waist, and perhaps a rifle in his hand. I suppose that by reason of their being so near the fort, they thought they were safe from attacks of Indians. Now they thought surely their time had come and crouched down in the grass and weeds to receive their doom. Newcomb gave a long, low whistle which must have been an inspiration, for the Indians turned and rode away without molesting them, evidently thinking the whistle was a signal to the soldiers.

They reached home and Newcomb went for his horse to give the alarm to soldiers and citizens, while Sister sat in the dark house alone for two and a half hours, afraid to make a light. She would hold her watch in the fireplace and strike a match to see the time. This was a long, tense wait with only the kitten, which she held in her lap, for company.

IX

Not very long after the war ended, there came to this country to seek his fortune a young Union soldier, Nathan L. Bartholomew of Connecticut. He was rather courageous to venture alone among people who were still sore over defeat, many of them feeling great bitterness and prejudice against anyone who wore the blue. He landed first in the little village of Pickettville, and was not too cordially received by the citizens as a whole, but the Matthews home opened its doors to him and he was kindly treated there. His first work was teaching a school in that home for the children of the village. From Picketville he came to Fort Griffin, taking a position in Newcomb's store as clerk, and from that time on was as one of us. While in the Army he acquired the nickname of "Barney" and that name clung to him ever after.

In the latter part of 1868, two of the Matthews girls, Mary and Martha, called "Mattie," came to stay with the Newcombs and attend school, while their brother, "Bud," as he was called by everyone, stayed with us. This school was taught by Mr. Tom Matthews, an uncle of these children. These schools, as I remember them, were of short duration and of the most elementary sort, yet they were an advantage to be taken.

One of my childhood memories of old Fort Griffin days is connected with the "apple wagons." Now and then in the fall and winter, a man would bring a wagon load of apples and peddle them out from house to house. How good that apple wagon did smell! Never since have any apples smelled half so nice. I do not remember now, if I ever knew, what they sold for. I do know that they brought such a fancy price that we did not get many tastes. I have read an article only recently where a man tells his experience with selling apples in Parker County in early days. He sold his at ten cents each, or ten dollars a bushel, and said his load netted him five hundred dollars. As we were much farther west, they were without doubt sold for more here. One of these apple men stayed in our home while he was retailing his apples. He had hauled his load all the way from Missouri and had to cross eight toll bridges on the way, so he needed to get a good price for his apples, he said.

In the early fall of 1869, after more than a year's absence, the young wanderer, Bennie, returned, to the great joy of all the family. He came home looking husky and fine, and had a very good stake to show for his year's work and his little bunch of cattle, as well as a wider outlook on life, having been in several of the western states and visited some of the larger cities, San Francisco, Sacramento and Salt Lake City, which meant a great deal in the way of an education to one of his age.

In coming home, he traveled part of the way by rail, part by stage, and finished his journey on horseback, buying his two horses at the end of the stage line, packing his belongings on one and riding the other. On the route he passed near a tavern kept by a family named B——, and it seems providential that he did not stop for the night at this house, for it was later revealed that it was a den of robbers and murderers.

5 *Parker County*

THIS WINTER OF 1869 saw another break in the family as my father decided to move into a more settled part of the country. It was the first of December when we set out for our new home, this time going to Parker County, near Weatherford. Only three of the children were now with the parents, the two younger boys, Glenn and Phin, and I. The Newcombs stayed on at Fort Griffin, Bennie remaining with them. All this moving was nothing more than a lark for me, for I enjoyed all trips of this kind. On the way we spent one or two nights with friends, and gathered pecans some mornings before going on. Nothing exciting happened until the last night out, not many miles from Weatherford. That night the Indians came into our camp and took two of my father's horses, and two belonging to others of the party. They did this so quietly and easily that no one was disturbed, and we knew nothing of their visit until the next morning when we got up and found the horses gone and the moccasin tracks in the sand very near where we slept. Some of the horses were tied up to the wagons, and if they had not been, I presume we would have been set afoot.

We went first to the home of our relative, Uncle Sam Barber, who lived on a farm four miles west of Weatherford. We visited with them a few days, then established ourselves in a small tenant house on the place until Father could look about for a farm to his liking. He soon found a very good one for sale, well improved, with a house that was considered the best of farmhouses in that country, although that did not mean much. We were so anxious to take possession and get things going that we moved in early in the spring before the former owners had vacated. It was a frame and clapboard house, ceiled inside, but unpainted. Father painted it white outside with green trim and it looked very attractive. The yard with its grassy lawn, shade trees and a sprinkle of shrubbery appealed to me, and a big cherry tree on the east side was an object of beauty when in bloom. There was a nice peach orchard and a vegetable garden, and there were plums and dewberries in the woods. All these were a pleasant change from the more arid west.

So my father again took up the life of a farmer. I think the main idea of this move was the hope of having better schools for us younger children. While the schools were more regular, perhaps, and with longer terms, they were only country schools at that, and no great improvement over what we had had on the Clear Fork. As for the social side of life, my mother did not consider it as good as that which she had forsaken at Fort Griffin. We had left dear ones behind us, my sister, brother, brother-in-law and dear little nephew, and we were homesick for them, for the broad prairies and that old river on the banks of which the first nine years of my childhood had been spent.

Farm life is very different from ranch life in every way. On a ranch there is so much more color and movement and so many more people. When one has been used to from ten to fifteen people coming and going, a quiet farm seems lonely and humdrum, and although I was too young then to think much about that, I did miss what I had been accustomed to. I have said the work was harder for all. Perhaps the cooking may have been less at times, but at harvest and threshing time, in fact, at all times, there is work in plenty for the farmer's wife.

II

As I have said, the Newcomb family stayed on at Fort Griffin, and Sam had started to build up a ranch on a little creek near where the town of Albany now stands. This creek is called Newcomb for him. As he had to be away from home a part of the time while he was building his ranch house, he moved his family down into the Flat by the Fort and boarded them with a Mrs. Frans, not my mother's friend of that name, but one who took her place after she had died. Barney Bartholomew ran the store while Newcomb was looking after his ranch business, and my brother, Ben, was helping with the ranch work.

At this time there came an epidemic of measles through the whole country and they were all stricken. Newcomb got out too soon and went to work in the store unpacking goods. He became overheated and wet with a heavy perspiration which was followed by a chill, and this promising young life was snuffed out like a candle.

I might say in passing that we on the farm in Parker County did not escape this epidemic; we were stricken, too. There was a large household as the family from which we bought had not yet moved out. There was a plague of measles in that house, six cases. They kept us shut up almost air-tight and fed us on hot teas, toddies, soups and the like. How sick we were! I wonder that we all survived, but we did and came out without any bad consequences. There was a family in a tenant house on the place where the mother had measles as well as the children. She being sick in bed and not able to keep the children in, they ran in and out with doors wide open as it was springtime, and they were none of them very ill. They hardly stayed in bed at all. Incidentally, two of these children, Jim and Cassie Savage, had at one time been captives of the Indians.

Now there had to be an adjustment of affairs in my sister's life. Father went back to Fort Griffin to look after her, and they disposed of everything, store, ranch and cattle. Sister and her little son came home to live with us and, of course, were welcomed with open arms.

III

Life went on in the usual way with farmers, seed time and harvest, school when convenient for the farmers. Our schoolhouse was about two miles away; we walked most of the time but some of the time we would ride. I would ride behind Phin on a pony and it was not unusual for me to tumble off two or three times on the way coming or going. Here I had as a friend and associate a young cousin of my age, Georgia McLean, daughter of the young man who went across the plains to Colorado and granddaughter of Uncle Sam Barber. We became lifelong friends.

In the summer there were camp meetings where we would join the neighbors in a camp of several days, with revival services held under a large arbor of green brush. Several families would pitch their tents together, and cook and eat together. All this was one big picnic to the children and was thoroughly enjoyed. We took pleasure in it all, especially the shouting and singing. Those old camp meetings were a part of every summer in that time and were looked forward to as a pleasant break in the monotony of the farmer's life. There would be visiting among the campers between the religious services, although sunrise prayer meeting, services at nine and eleven o'clock in the morning, at three in the afternoon, vespers at sundown and services at "early candlelight" were calculated to keep people rather well employed.

These old-fashioned camp meetings have gone out of date almost entirely in this day of rush and hurry. There is one, however, that deserves "honorable mention," the famous "Fort Davis Camp Meeting," more generally known as the "Bloys" or "Cowboy Camp Meeting." It was organized in 1889 by Dr. Bloys, a Presbyterian home missionary located at Fort Davis, and a few ranchmen and their families, only about twenty people in all. They were the families of George Evans, C. O. Finley, W. T. Jones, John Means, George Medley and Jesse Merrill. Brother George was one of the founders but was not present at the first meeting.

The first services were held under a large live-oak tree which is still standing and is used now by the Evans and Means camp as a dining arbor. The camp ground is located in Skillman's Grove, a beautiful live-oak grove in a valley in the Davis mountains. The grove, with its surroundings of mountain peaks, is undoubtedly one of the most lovely spots in all of this big state. Dr. Bloys, called "the Sky Pilot" by those who knew and loved him, has gone to his reward as have several others who were at that first meeting. A number of the old faithfuls are left and they with their children and grandchildren, who have become a host, together with many new ones, gather at this camp ground each year in the first part of August to worship God amid the beauties of nature. To attend that camp meeting and mingle with those people is indeed a privilege.

The old brush arbor has given way to a tabernacle that seats near a thousand and there are water and electric light systems now, but the same old spirit of friendliness and western hospitality prevails. While all the founders that are left are in the evening time of life and will not be there many more years, their children and grandchildren are following in their footsteps and carrying on, having been trained in the way.

Although it occurred a number of years later, I shall mention our first attendance at this meeting because it is an example of the whole-hearted spirit of the west. In 1903, we, with almost our entire family, made a visit to the Reynolds Brothers' ranch in the Fort Davis Mountains. This ranch had been acquired some years before and was far away from the other ranches of the family in Texas, being almost on the border line of Southwest Texas, more than three hundred miles away from us. Brother George, wanting to give it some intriguing name, as this was his special find and a ranch that delighted his soul, called it "South Africa" because it was so far away. As this ranch is in the mountains, it has a delightful summer climate and became a family resort. They keep open house practically all the time while spending the summer there, and with such a large family connection and many friends, they have a rather full house most of the time. There is a fine orchard with plums, peaches, apples and pears, and a vineyard with a varied assortment of grapes. Water flowing from cool springs makes this an oasis, indeed.

We went out the first of August on this, our first, visit. After a few days at the ranch, preparations were on to attend the Fort Davis Camp Meeting, a distance of ninety miles around the mountains the way we went. Everything in the way of a hack, buggy and buckboard was brought into requisition, everyone on the ranch going except a Mexican who was left to look after the place. We started out, with tow wagons carrying the equipage, each drawn by four horses. All the cowboys, visiting young men, and some of the girls rode horseback, some fifteen or twenty of them. So, with the buggies and other vehicles, we had quite a train. At noontime we were joined by another ranch outfit, that of Mr. Tatum, a neighbor. The first night we reached Mr. G. W. Evans' ranch in Panther Canyon, a most beautiful, picturesque spot, but lonely looking as it is so deep in the hills. Here we stretched tents and made camp; Mr. Evans had a beef already barbecued when we got there. They had a house full and overflowing with guests who were all bound for the camp meeting. That night the younger Evans boys who were little fellows then, led by big Jake, the colored cook, put on a show for us.

The next morning we set out again, almost a hundred strong. This day we drove to the Means Ranch near Valentine; it was in the open prairie where one could see far away. Here again there was a beef barbecued and we were entertained in the evening with the Evans and Means orchestra.

The next morning when we took the road, the party had increased to one hundred and thirty. When we arrived on a hill overlooking the camp grounds in late afternoon, a glorious sight met our eyes. The lovely valley with its groves of live-oak trees nestling under the shelter of rugged mountains, with the soft shades of evening coming on, was a view to delight the eye of an artist. Now we were on a gentle slope of a half mile; here Brother George got out of his buggy, commandeered a horse and marshalled the train in military order. Mr. and Mrs. Evans' buggy with a beautiful pair of cream colored horses led the van, followed by all the lighter vehicles, then came the horseback riders by twos and they had increased since the first start. Bringing up the rear were the seven camp wagons. Altogether we made a rather imposing company and added materially to the crowd on the camp grounds. The Evans and Means had their regular camping place and assigned us a spot on which to stretch our tents. The mess wagons were placed side by side in a semicircle near the camp fire with the mess boxes, which were in the backs of the wagons, next to the fire.

Dr. Bloys, the founder of this meeting was still there when we made our first visit. He was a rather small man, looking very much like a cowboy in his Stetson hat and with his modest, unassuming manner. We soon found, however, that though small in stature he was a giant in ability and forcefulness, and ruled every detail of this vast encampment, which ran like clockwork.

There was no selling nor bartering on these grounds; everything was free. A meal could not be bought. There was a fund for general expenses, buying the beef and other things, and each camp was self-supporting. Each of these ranchmen who camped together furnished his share and, of course, all visitors wanted to help defray the expenses of the camp though they all were welcomed; the hospitality of these campers was unbounded. There was much pleasant social intercourse between services when old friendships were renewed and new ones made, but there was no boisterousness; everything moved in the most dignified manner. As I said in the beginning, they were there primarily to worship God.

IV

The late fall of 1870 is a notable one in the Reynolds family and interest picks up greatly, for it marks the return of our wanderers, Brother George and Sister Bettie and Will, and brings the family together once more. There was rejoicing in the home, and their coming was like a fairy's dream to this child. They appeared grand and prosperous, bringing beautiful gifts from California's golden shores. Sister Bettie, dressed handsomely in costumes made by city dressmakers, seemed the grand lady indeed. They had spent a good part of the past year in San Francisco and other cities, and from this time on, the lives of this young couple were almost like a bit from *The Arabian Nights*, they were so interesting and colorful.

One day soon after they came, a big ambulance drawn by a fine pair of mules was driven up to our door and who should that be but the Matthews family, as "welcome as flowers in May."

The driver was Bud, who had grown into a handsome young man with a well developed mustache, a real heart-breaker at eighteen. This family had been on an extended visit with relatives in Louisiana and they had timed their arrival to meet the daughter whom they had not seen in more than two years, and they were long years to those who were left behind. Having sold their cattle interests out West, they were taking a sabbatical year of vacation, so they located themselves temporarily in our tenant house until such time as they could decide on a permanent location. This arrangement was very pleasing to me as there were two girls in the family near my age, my birthday being half-way between Mattie's and Susie's. They were there several months and we went to school together, played together and had good times as carefree children will.

The farm became a lively place this winter. Brother George was assembling a cow outfit, getting ready to move some cattle in the spring. These men went into camp as the houses were full and running over. There were some musicians among them; Henry Fosdick was expert with the banjo while Mart Bowie could whistle and sing to Henry's accompaniment. He whistled *The Mocking-Bird* to perfection; his whistling sounded just like that we hear over the radio now. Sister Bettie had brought an accordion home with her and everyone, big and little, was trying that out. Brother Will possessed a flute and could play that a little, but the banjo and the whistler were in demand every evening when the family gathered in the farmhouse.

This winter, I remember, I read my first novel, being in my tenth year. It was *Pickwick Papers*. From then on I was a voracious reader, reading everything that came my way except dime novels, for they were strictly forbidden. When there was a mixed bunch of men around, there usually would be a few such thrillers lying around; they were called "yellow backs" then. I grant you they were no worse than many of the movies indulged in now.

Among the cowboys that were assembled here was a young man late from California who had fallen in with my brothers somewhere, Mart Gentry, one of Nature's noblemen whom to know was to love. He became associated with them from this time until his death a few years ago.

v

This winter was spent by Brother George in going about the country, contracting for cattle. When spring opened, the cattle were brought together in a place called "Lost Valley" in Jack County, near the Loving Ranch. As I remember it, this place became rather noted for Indian raids. There were two camps here, Brother's outfit with one herd being about a mile away from one that was in charge of Charley Rivers, a son-in-law of Mr. Oliver Loving, before mentioned. As my brother had bought the latter herd and was to receive it the next morning, he was spending the night in the camp with Rivers. Some time in the night an alarm was raised; Indians were raiding the camp and driving the horses off. All jumped up, there was great excitement and confusion in the dark, and in the melée Charley Rivers was shot, no one knew whether by his own men or the Indians. He was taken into Weatherford as soon as possible for medical treatment, but he was mortally wounded and did not live long, lingering for a few weeks only.

When daylight came, they found the Indians had taken all the horses except those the night herders were riding. The horses were some distance from the cattle which were not disturbed. Real Indians did not care so much about cattle; it was horses that they were after. The next day Mr. Jim Loving sold them a fresh supply of horses from the Loving Ranch, near-by, and the cattle were received and started on the long drive to Colorado for their first winter. Brother Will had charge of one of the herds and Bennie went along with him. The other was bossed by a one-armed man, Rice Derrett, long since gone over the Great Divide. Mart Gentry was also with this herd.

Such herds of cattle had to be watched by night as well as day. Usually they would lie quietly all night unless disturbed, but sometimes a very slight, unusual noise would startle them, and then there was danger of a stampede, which was something to be dreaded. When a stampede once started, the cattle were beyond control. They would run at breakneck speed, and woe to anything in their way. The only thing the boys could do when that happened was to run along by the side of the herd, pressing close to the cattle until they would gradually get them turned and going in a circle, letting them run until they ran themselves down. Sometimes a storm in the night would start them and then it was even more serious trying to quiet them with rain and, perhaps, hail pelting down. A stampede did not occur often as there always would be three or four men riding around them all night. Frequently it would be very difficult for the night herders to stay awake. Some would even put chewing tobacco in their eyes to keep them from going to sleep, and it was a very effective method. They would whistle and sing to the cattle and the cattle, being used to hearing their voices and the movement of the horses, would lie contented.

As John A. Lomax poetically puts it:

> *What keeps the herd from running,*
> *Stampeding far and wide?*
> *The cowboy's long, low whistle,*
> *And singing by their side.*

Herds on the trail were kept in touch with each other as much as possible for mutual help and protection. They did this even when the cattle were not owned by one man, but more especially if one man had two herds. The lead herd would be kept a mile or so in advance to keep the cattle from mixing. The reason the cattle were driven in two bunches was that they were more easily handled in that way, but, of course, dividing the herd required more men, wagons and horses. There were men who sometimes would drive as many as three or four thousand in one herd, but as a rule they would not have over two thousand. For a herd of one or two thousand, there often would be two wagons or more, eight to twelve men and about forty horses. The wagons and horses were usually in front of the cattle. One man, called the "wrangler," took care of the horses. If they were in a part of the country where Indians were not too numerous, the men with the horses and wagons sometimes would go on several miles ahead to locate water and make camp, in which case the cook would have the meal prepared when the herd got to camp, but most of the time the whole outfit would keep close together. The cattle would be allowed to rest and graze an hour or two at noon, then they would stop early in the afternoon if water and grass were plentiful, and the cattle would graze until dark, when they would lie down to rest and sleep.

The reason they had so many horses, each man having three or four, was that they would usually change horses at noon and always take a fresh horse every morning. Each man retained one horse for night guard only and this horse was kept saddled and ready at night as it took too much time from their sleeping hours to catch and saddle horses. One shift would come into camp and quietly awaken the next guard, whereupon they would get up and mount their horses which were standing ready, saddled and bridled, without disturbing the camp. They spent little time in dressing, as about all they would take off would be their hats and boots. Some days when they found good grass and water, they would rest several hours; then the boys could have a bath and wash their clothes.

While these drives were long and tiresome, they were not without interest and excitement to one who was making his first trip. There was an element of danger, not only from Indians but from other things as well. Scarcity of water was a serious hazard, sometimes man and beast perished for want of water on the drives, but that did not happen often. There was always the spirit of adventure which appealed to young men, and they were ever ready to undertake the drive on the trail.

The final goal for most of these herds was California, that Golden State, where in those early days fabulous prices were often realized from a herd of beef steers. The herds were of that class of cattle, nearly altogether. It took two seasons to bring a herd into California from Texas as cattle are slow moving creatures; ten to twelve miles a day was about the limit, and many days they would not make that. Some days, though, when they had been without water for a stretch of thirty miles they would travel faster, and when they came near enough to water to smell it, they would break into a run and there was no holding them back. They could smell it for miles, too, when they were starving for it.

Although it occurred over twenty years later, I shall mention an incident here because it exemplifies one of the varied difficulties encountered by trail herds. In the intervening years, Reynolds Brothers had incorporated under the name of Reynolds Cattle Company, most of the family and Mart Gentry taking stock in the company. Phin was driving some cattle to Dakota for the company when he had an unfortunate experience, as you will see. The Reynolds cattle were in two divisions, or herds, which were some ten miles apart, and in between them were four other herds belonging to another cattle company, the XIT. The reason the two Reynolds herds were separated, with one in front and the other behind these other herds of a different brand, was because the four XIT herds, which had been in the lead and driven hard, had become footsore and weary and were lagging behind. Phin had had Tom Matthews, who was boss of the front herd of Reynolds cattle, to ease his herd to the front, going around the four herds; the other herd would have followed his lead the next day but for the disaster revealed in the following telegram from Phin.

JUNE 2, 1892

A SNOWSTORM STRUCK US ON THE HIGH DIVIDE FIFTY MILES EAST OF DENVER COLORADO. TWENTY-EIGHT HEAD OF HORSES FROZEN TO DEATH. SIX HERDS IN ONE AND DRIFTED THIRTY MILES SOUTH. FRESH HORSES HERE. MEN ALL ACCOUNTED FOR.

P. W. REYNOLDS.

The new horses had been sent from Dakota to meet them and reached them the day before the storm, which was fortunate, for they, being fresh and strong from a cold climate, did not freeze. The horses that they had been using were old and were to be sent back home when the fresh horses came, but the storm did not leave many.

Now here was what might be called "a pretty kettle of fish," fifteen thousand head of cattle of different brands all mixed in one bunch and strayed thirty miles south of the road. It took the men six days to round them up and separate the different brands, and I think they did well to get it done in that length of time, for besides the trail herds, the local cattle of that part of the country were mixed in. There were only eight head of the Reynolds brand missing while the other company lost three hundred, most of them frozen to death. They had been driven too hard and were jaded. These trail herds had to move slowly, and not every man put in charge of one knew how to handle it.

VI

After seeing the herds off, Brother George and Sister Bettie left for Colorado, taking Glenn and Bud with them. They were driven to Fort Gibson, Indian Territory, in the Matthews ambulance, the driver being a little Frenchman whom we called "Frenchie." He looked very important that morning standing by his team with his big gauntlets on. At Fort Gibson they took a train and were landed at Kit Carson, Colorado. From there they went over to the Arkansas River where they found a place that looked like a bonanza to my brother. On the north side of the river, some years before this, the Government had opened up an irrigation project, and had made a ditch large enough to furnish water for several hundred acres of land. They also had built the walls of two good stone houses. The plan of our Government had been to put the Indians on this reservation and teach them farming, to try to civilize them and make citizens of them. The War Between the States came on and this project was abandoned.

In 1863, one General Chivington with his detachment of troops massacred a band of seven hundred of these same Cheyenne Indians, mostly women and children. This wholesale slaughter took place between Kit Carson and the Arkansas River in what is now Kiowa County, and there is a station on the Missouri-Pacific named "Chivington." However, I am glad to say that the Army did not keep General Chivington; he was cashiered for this act of brutality. For some reason nothing more was done about putting the Indians on this reservation to teach them agriculture, and the improvements were abandoned by the Government.

The stone walls were left standing there between two hills, a very picturesque spot overlooking a large valley with the river curving around the south side. The place was called "Point of Rocks" and was an inviting location just waiting for someone with vision to take advantage of it, with its miles of open grazing land on the north, making a fine free range for cattle. This was Government land, subject to preemption in one hundred and sixty acre tracts with small easy payments. My brother, George, took steps at once to secure the valley with its splendid irrigation system, and preempted two tracts, one in his own name and one in Brother Will's, and began operations by finishing off the houses neatly. Twenty-five miles north on Adobe Creek, he built a small adobe house as a boundary camp. There were no pasture fences in those days; the land owned by the Government was open to any one for grazing until it was preempted by the actual settler. The only way to keep the cattle within a given territory was to establish what were called line camps. From an established point, two men going in opposite directions would ride out a certain distance each morning, turning the cattle back into the range, would meet a man from another camp, then go back over the same ground in the afternoon, turning the cattle in again. In this way they managed to keep the cattle fairly well located. These men were called line riders.

VII

For the two families on the farm in Parker County, life dropped back into the old routine. School was still in session and an incident of this session, long to be remembered, was a hail storm. One morning when we left for school, there was a dark cloud hanging in the west which looked ugly and threatening, but the mothers let us go on, thinking it would blow over, perhaps. Early in the afternoon that cloud came on with a rush! The teacher, Uncle Sam Barber, for some reason thought it best to leave the school building and go to the nearest farmhouse, a half mile away. I do not know why he should have run from the storm as we had shelter where we were. He marshalled the whole school out on the road and we set off in a run. We were hardly well under way before the storm broke and we were pounded by hail stones and rain all the way, reaching the farmhouse a bedraggled set of youngsters, but not much dampened in spirits. Now our part of the crowd was a half mile farther from home than at the schoolhouse, we having gone in the opposite direction. We did not enjoy the prospect of that extra half mile walk in the mud either, but pretty soon, up rode Father Matthews. He had mounted his horse and had come out to look for us. While we were debating what to do next, as we could not all ride the one horse, one of the girls, I think it was Mattie, looked down where the Weatherford road ran below the field and spied the ambulance. "There's Frenchie!" she cried, and our problem was solved. Father Matthews rode down and headed him our way. When we got into the ambulance, we found it well loaded with the largest apples we had ever seen, and we went home in great glee, for once having all the apples we could eat. No gilded chariot could ever have been more welcome than that ambulance was right then. Frenchie was getting home, after taking the folks to the railroad, and certainly appeared at the opportune time.

VIII

The year of 1871 was a notable one in the history of West Texas because of the capture and bringing to trial of a trio of Indians, Satanta, Satank and Big Tree. These three chiefs of the Kiowas had terrorized the border country for years, and were the dread of the citizens. They were truly bad Indians, wily and treacherous.

On May 17, a wagon train owned by a man named Warren, consisting of seven wagons and teamsters, set out from Fort Richardson at Jacksboro loaded with supplies for Fort Griffin, sixty miles to the west. Some hours later a terror stricken man came into Jacksboro; the train had been attacked by a large band of Indians, and he alone of the seven men had escaped death. Two of the teamsters had been chained beneath the wagons and burned.

General McKenzie was in Jacksboro at the time and immediately set out in pursuit. He soon came upon the scene of the massacre, saw the burned wagons and mutilated bodies of the victims, but the Indians had taken the mules and escaped. It so happened that General William T. Sherman was making a tour of inspection through West Texas, and the very day of the massacre, had come into Jacksboro from San Antonio, a fortunate coincidence for this country. A delegation of citizens waited upon him and laid the situation before him. General Sherman was impressed and, being a man of action, he hurried to Fort Sill, Indian Territory, where he conferred with Lawrie Tatum, Indian agent stationed there. And it was due to Sherman that these murderous chiefs were so speedily brought to justice, though it is doubtful if the guilty ones would have been found so quickly had it not been for big Chief Satanta's foolish pride. He was drunk with bloodshed and could not hold his peace, but had to strut before General Sherman and Tatum. He wanted it understood that, while Satank and Big Tree were with him on the raid, he, and he alone, was in command and all the glory was his. The poor braggart was taken at his word. General Sherman had seen and heard enough. He was a man of strong common sense as well as great military ability and he realized that the policy of kindness and gentleness which our Government was trying on the Indians these late years was a complete failure. Perhaps, had that policy been pursued in the early history of our country, the results might have been more successful; who knows? Now, at least some of these savages needed sterner measures to bring them into subjection, and Sherman was the man of the hour.

He immediately ordered the arrest of Santanta, Satank and Big Tree, and not many days after the massacre, they were on their way to Jacksboro, under military escort and heavily ironed. It was quick work when you consider the vast expanse of country and the slow mode of travel.

Satank never reached Jacksboro. It is said that he gnawed the flesh from his hand and slipped a handcuff, then grabbed a weapon and tried to kill one of the guards, when he was riddled with bullets. Before he did this, he made a loud harangue, telling Satanta and Big Tree that he was a warrior and a chief and not to be treated as a child. Then the guards heard a weird chant. They did not know it, but Satank was singing his death song. The words and translation of this song appeared in some newspaper stories of the episode, having been found, I think, in the diary of one of the officers. I shall quote them for what they may be worth.

> *I-ha hyo-o-ya o i-ha ya-ya yo-yo*
> *Kai-tsenko ana-obahe-ma haa-ipat-degi o-ba-ika*
> *A-he-ya a-he-ya ya-he-yo ya e-ya he-yo e-hi-yo*
> *Kai-tsenko- ana-obahe-ma ha-da-mga-gi o-ba-ika.*
>
> *O, Sun, you remain forever,*
> *But we, Kaitsenko, must die;*
> *O, Earth, you remain forever,*
> *But we, Kaitsenko, must die.*

They loaded his body onto a wagon and sent it back to Fort Sill. Satanta and Big Tree were brought on to town.

Never before in the history of this western country had a wild Indian been brought before a white man's court for trial. With the border citizens wrought up to the highest pitch of excitement and rage, this trial must have been a strain and a good bit of a burlesque, though it was conducted with due order and solemnity throughout. The citizens, heavily armed, crowded the courthouse and yard, but managed to contain their bitter resentment.

The chiefs were indicted for murder and tried before Judge Charles Soward of the 13th, now 43rd, Judicial District, S. W. T. Lanham, father of Congressman Fritz Lanham and later governor of Texas, was the prosecuting attorney. It is said that his oratory on this occasion brought him into political prominence.

Satanta was an orator himself, and a wise one. At the close of the trial he was allowed to speak for himself, but most of his talk consisted of straight-out lies. He posed as the friend of the white man and as very innocent of any crimes against Texans, "had never been so near Tehannas before," etc., etc. He promised that if they would let him go free, he would avenge the massacre and wash out all the blood with the blood of the guilty Indians. "But if you kill me," he said, "it will be a spark on the prairie, make big fire heap burn."

His speech compelled attention and admiration for a few moments, but the evidence was too strong against the Indians. They were convicted of murder and sentenced to be hanged. The sentence was never executed; after thinking over Satanta's speech, Judge Soward decided there really was some truth in what he had said about the spark of fire, and he feared a conflagration might be brought on that would be hard to control. Therefore, he recommended to Governor Davis that their sentences be commuted to life imprisonment. They were sent to the state penitentiary at Huntsville, but they were not there for long, for influence was brought to bear on the powers at Washington, and after two years, Satanta and Big Tree were out on parole.

Big Tree had learned a lesson and reformed, became a Christian and joined the Church, lived to a good old age and died a short time ago, a respected citizen of Oklahoma.

Satanta returned to his old way of life, depredating on the border, and was again arrested and sent back to the penitentiary where he committed suicide by throwing himself from a third story window. The confinement was more than his wild spirit could endure.

It so happened that Bud Matthews was traveling on the same stage with these chiefs for part of the journey to the penitentiary. He said that he sat on the box with the driver some of the time; the driver was drunk and drove under a bois d'arc tree, one of the limbs knocking his hat off. Bud finally got inside the coach with the Indians where he almost smothered in tobacco smoke as the Indians kept their clay pipes going constantly.

IX

This summer of 1871, after my brothers had gone to Colorado, Sister decided to take her little son, Gus, to visit his father's people who lived in Missouri, near Chillicothe. This was quite an undertaking in those days for one who had never been over a hundred miles from home in her life, the trip from Fort Griffin to Weatherford being the extent of her travels. The journey was made partly by stage and partly by train; Texas at that time did not have many miles of rails. She went by stage to Fort Scott, Kansas, and there she took the train to Chillicothe, Missouri, where she spent the summer with the Newcomb family.

In the fall she went out to Colorado to visit Brother George and Sister Bettie and the others of the family there. They were spending the winter in Pueblo where Brother George had bought a nice home, and they had with them the two young brothers, Bud and Glenn, who were attending school there. This winter was marked by illness for those of the family in Colorado. Brother George had a serious attack of pneumonia, Gus had inflammatory rheumatism, and to cap everything else, William, who had come up from the ranch at Point of Rocks for a little visit, while exploring the new home, opened the cellar door and, not realizing that he was going into a cellar, fell all the way to the bottom where he struck an ironbound keg. He cut his face so badly on it that he had to have several stitches taken and was laid up for some time.

After all were well again, they had a jolly time through the remainder of the winter. Bartholomew was there part of the time and was very much interested in the young widow. In fact, suitors were rather plentiful at this time.

In the meantime, the two herds of cattle had been brought safely through with no more attacks by Indians, one stopping in a place called "Salt Bottom" on the Arkansas River near the line of Colorado, where the cattle were kept for the winter; the other was taken on to the ranch at Point of Rocks.

In the spring of 1872, the two herds were on the move again. One of them, which had been sold to a man named Hoyt, was put in the charge of Bennie, a youngster just twenty years old at that time. The other was in the care of Bud Matthews, who was only nineteen. They were young to have been placed in such responsible positions, but were quite equal to the occasion and carried these herds safely to the state of Nevada on the Humboldt River, where Mr. Hoyt took his over. The other herd had been sold, too, but the buyer backed out of his trade and the cattle were left on their hands for awhile. They finally traded them for horses and made a profit in that way.

As I have said before, California was the goal of most of the cattle from Texas at this time, and these herds probably reached there ultimately, though our folks left them in Nevada. The outfits took charge of the horses there and drove them back to the ranch in Colorado. Ben and Bud, however, went on to San Francisco where, they say, they saw more gold than they had

THE JOSEPH BECK MATTHEWS HOUSE,
*eighteen miles from Reynolds Bend, was
built in 1874 or 1875 near old Fort Griffin.*

ever thought there was in the country. Gold was the current money of the time, everything was paid in gold. There would be sacks of it sitting around in the banks and in Wells Fargo express offices. It was rightly called the Golden State.

X

When Sister came home in the early spring, she found a change in our neighborhood, for in the fall of 1871 the Matthews family left us. They bought a ranch on the Clear Fork six miles east of Fort Griffin, moved there and began improving the place. The ranch home was built of logs to begin with, but that house burned and was replaced by one of cut sandstone. The home, situated near the river among beautiful live-oak trees, was known as "Pleasant View" because the surroundings and general outlook were so delightful to the eye.

Sister had a very pleasant and profitable visit; seeing new places and mixing with new people is an asset. Young men were dropping in at the farmhouse rather often now. Bartholomew, who had been in Colorado for the winter, was soon back in Texas. While he was not in Parker County, he was not far away, and a lively correspondence was in progress between him and my sister. It was evident that he was the favored suitor, and soon she informed me that I was to have a new brother, the same being this young Yankee soldier. I had not seen much of him up to that time, and did not yet know him very well. Being a hot-headed little rebel, I was a bit resentful of this Northerner and asked Sister if she could do such a dreadful thing as to marry a man who had fought against her own brother. She only laughed at my childish explosion, and wedding preparations did not cease because of my objections.

In due time, the marriage was celebrated in a double ceremony in which my brother, Will, was married to Mary Byrd, a sweet, lovely girl who died six months later in Colorado. I learned to love this dear Brother Barney as I did my very own brothers. They were married in the summer and left in a short time for Eastland County where Brother Barney had bought a farm and established a small ranch. Years afterward, rich oil wells were developed on this place, but it had long since passed out of his hands.

Now the only children left in the home nest were Phin and I. All the rest had gone, and some far afield, at least, Colorado seemed far away in that day and time. My father felt an urge to see the boys in that new country, and in the fall of 1872, he sold his farm for cash, getting more than double what he had paid for it, this being a very fortunate sale for him. We made ready to move again. Winter was not a good time of the year to change to a colder clime, but the decision was made and the farm sold. I think Mother was very willing to leave the farm, as she thought we would be going back to ranch life. Brother Barney came down with team and wagon to help move us to the end of the railroad, the Missouri, Kansas and Texas, which was then reaching into Texas, the terminus being just across the river from Denison.

Colorado

I

W<small>E LEFT WEATHERFORD</small> on the 23rd of November, 1872, and drove to Colbert's Ferry
on Red River, taking two or three days for
this trip. The last night out, we camped in the Indian Territory
near where the railroad ended then. We had crossed on the
ferry-boat and two of us had left Texas soil for the first time in
our lives, an exciting event for Phin and me. The next morning
a passenger train pulled in and came to a standstill right there
in the tall timber. There was not so much as a section house
there, not anything, just the rails. There may have been a section
house back a few miles, but I do not remember anything but
that train now, and it looked most interesting. We were loaded
on, with our trunks and boxes; we were not taking any furniture,
only a few books and some china. This was my first sight of a
train, and the Pullman appeared very elegant and comfortable,
heated by big coal stoves in each end and lighted by coal-oil
lamps which were the first coal-oil or kerosene lamps I had ever
seen. We were still using candles on the farm, but candles of
sperm and wax which were an improvement on the tallow dips
my mother had made. The coal-oil lamps gave a much brighter
light than candles; in fact, with a shade they gave an excellent
light for reading. Those old Pullmans that looked so grand then

would seem crude and antiquated now, but they were pioneers, as were we.

We went to Junction City, Kansas, on the Missouri, Kansas and Texas, where we had a tiresome wait of several hours in the station before being transferred to the Kansas Pacific, now a part of the Union Pacific system, which took us to Kit Carson, Colorado, sixty miles from our destination. Here we had a good night's rest at the hotel, and the next morning arranged for transportation to the ranch. We were late getting started and were heavily loaded, and it was in the night when we came to the ranch on Adobe Creek. This little house with its chimney in one corner seemed cozy and warm when we got there after a slow thirty-five mile drive in the cold. We found Colorado much colder than Texas, that is, the section where we lived. A young man, Jim Orchard, and his wife were the ranch keepers here, and they gave us supper and made us comfortable for the night. The next morning we were soon on our way again, and had not gone many miles when we were met by Bud with a team and light hack from the ranch. Then we moved out with some speed over those splendid natural roads that were almost like pavement, while the baggage wagon followed on at a slower pace. The day was fine and the air as bracing as wine.

II

When we drove up to Point of Rocks, the place looked grand to me. I thought the two white stone houses in their setting of hills were about the nicest things I had ever seen.

Life here was very different from that on the farm in Parker County. Here the people were more progressive and up to date. While there were some from all parts of the country, East, West, North and South, they were mostly from the northern states. A group of people from Texas whom we had known in old Fort

Davis, the Anderson family, had located just across the river. In those days, people from the North and East were inclined to look upon Texas people as only a few generations above the ape, and would even express surprise that really nice people should have come from Texas! As the Jews of old believed that no good thing could come out of Nazareth, so many in those early days believed that no good people could come out of Texas. As I said in the beginning of this history, Texas had a hard name, especially the western section of the state, being the refuge for criminals from all parts of the country, although some of the best blood of both North and South was represented in the founders of Texas. A remark that Sallie Reynolds was a *nice* girl to have come from Texas, with a rising inflection on the "Texas," was repeated to me. Any slur on Texas was resented by me in those days; I always rose in arms ready to defend my native state. However, I am a believer in people passing for what they are worth. Sometimes, of course, there are people who are not appreciated, but as a rule, if we are worthy of respect, we get it; but we must merit, not demand it.

Soon after we came out, Bud Matthews left for his home in Texas, and we did not see him any more for sometime. This winter we spent with Brother George and Sister Bettie in their home. They had accumulated a very nice little library in their travels and I reveled in that. My mother, who was deeply religious, had instilled in me a reverence for the Bible; from the time I was seven years old I was required to read it regularly, and this winter I became really interested in it. They also had a cottage organ and that was a source of pleasure to me; though I knew nothing of music, it was fun to pick out tunes by ear.

Point of Rocks was somewhat isolated; there were no near neighbors on our side of the river. Often the river would be full of mush ice in winter, and in spring there would be freshets from the snow melting in the mountains. However, it would be fordable most of the time and often we crossed when it was very deep. The social center for this part of the country was at Rocky Ford on the south side of the river, twelve miles above Point of Rocks. There Mr. Russell, the leading citizen, had a general merchandise business, and there was a post office, blacksmith shop and a small hotel. Soon after we came, the Russells had a dance in their home and there I made my bow to society. I was under thirteen, but my elder brothers and their wives were kind enough to take me with them. Here we met the "elite" of the surrounding country, and very pleasant people they were, who showed themselves friendly to the strangers in their midst, even though we were from Texas. I thoroughly enjoyed this party and many others.

There were three girls in the Russell family, two of them, Gustie and Annie, being near enough my age to be congenial. They would come down now and then to spend a few days with me, and would have me in their home for visits of days at a time. There was another girl of my age, Laura Potter, and we were together quite a bit. The Potters were a Missouri family and very genial.

Rocky Ford was our post office, and there would be passing back and forth; we did not get our mail every day by any means, once a week, perhaps, or not so often. There would be several dances during the winter months, some at the hotel and some at the Russell home, and we always attended. I was well chaperoned, usually by four brothers. A girl seldom had to sit out a dance in those days, even though only thirteen or fourteen, for the young men were very much in the majority.

We had an unusual experience one time when we were on our way to a dance at Rocky Ford. We were crossing the river near the ranch where the ford was rather deep when one of the horses deliberately sat down on his haunches in the water. Ben was driving and he chirruped, used his whip and did everything he could to get the horse up. No sir, old "George" just sat there as though there was nothing else in life. Getting to the party was no worry of his. Finally Phin got out, he being the youngest, such jobs usually falling on the younger boys of a family. He waded into the water waist deep, unfastened the tugs and worked with the horse. After plunging around awhile, taking all the time he wanted, the horse slowly got to his feet, the tugs were fastened, and we pulled out of the river at last. Now, of course, Phin had to go back home, only a little way. I felt very grieved over his having to miss the party; he was my chum, and aside from that he was wet and cold. That boy did not let so small a thing keep him from the party. He ran home, catching his pony on the way, changed his clothes, and when we got to Rocky Ford, there he was, as pert as you please, to my great joy. We had gone by another ranch to pick up a fiddler while he had gone a nearer route and without doubt had run his pony most of the way.

III

The next spring my father filed on a tract of land in this valley, about a mile from the main ranch but under the irrigation system. Here he built a small adobe house and opened up a farm. There is a certain kind of soil used in making these 'dobes. It is made into mortar, mixed with straw and cast into molds about eight by eight by sixteen inches. After standing in the molds until firm, the bricks or blocks are turned out and allowed to bake in the sun. I imagine they are the same kind over which the Israelites toiled while slaves in Egypt. The adobe houses are very common all through the arid West, Texas, New Mexico, Colorado and California, and they are quite comfortable, warm in winter and cool in summer.

The adobe soil is very productive. Raising crops by irrigation was a new experience to my father. While everything grew luxuriantly and the vegetables were luscious, I have never wanted anything to do with irrigation on an extensive scale; a garden or small truck patch is all right, but for a farm of any size, it is pure drudgery. Of course, any kind of farming means work, but I prefer the farm that is watered from above.

This summer Father had a good crop and the corn was just coming into roasting ear when an army of grasshoppers came over like a cloud and settled in the field. In a few hours there was nothing left except the stalks of the corn standing like stumps. The other farmers in the country all had the same loss. I think this was the same year that Kansas was so devastated by hoppers, but I am not certain about that.

The winter of 1873-4, my father employed a governess as there was no school near us. The people all lived on the south side of the river; the nearest ranch on the north side was eight miles down at old Bents Fort, a cattle ranch belonging to John Prowers at this time. Up the river there was no one for miles, I do not know how far now. Our teacher was a Miss Molly McGaughy, an efficient young woman from Illinois. Glenn, Phin and I had lessons with her this year. We did attend school across the river later on and had to ride horseback to and from it.

IV

In the spring of 1874, Brother and Sister Bettie made a visit to Texas, and when they came back, they brought Susie Matthews with them. That was a grand surprise for me and I was wild with joy at having this friend and playmate from Texas with me. We were together constantly at one home or the other. One of our main recreations was riding horseback; we did a lot of that. Sometimes we would race our horses and now and then would tumble off, but we were very fortunate in not being hurt. We seemed always to be able to find amusement, for our tastes were simple and easily satisfied. Then too, we had household tasks to employ our time.

The river abounded in fish, mostly a small narrow white fish, very good for eating. Sister Bettie had a maid of all work who loved fishing, and she would go to the river with us where we would fish in the quiet pools for hours, and often bring in dozens of these small fish, with an occasional drum or some other larger fish, which was rare.

For awhile this summer we attended a little school across the river. There did not seem to be much regularity about these country schools; they would be in session most any time in the year for a short term. This particular school was taught by Hiram Barber, son of Uncle Sam Barber. The schoolhouse was across the river and two or three miles up. We rode horseback, Phin, Susie and I, a boy from the ranch, and Hiram, who lived with us. One evening when school closed and we went out to get our horses, we could not find a one. They had gone home and left us afoot, so there was nothing to do but walk home. When we came to the river which we had to cross, the boys pulled off their shoes to wade and carry us. Susie said, "I want Phin to carry me." I was quite willing to have Hiram transport me because he was a grown man and, I thought, a little safer than my lad brother. The water was not very deep at this ford and we were soon safely landed on the home side, while the other boy, whose name I cannot remember now, brought over books, lunch baskets and shoes.

V

In the fall of 1874, the Kansas Pacific railroad built across from Kit Carson to the Arkansas River, where they established West Las Animas on the south side of the river. It was called

"West Las Animas" because there was a town named "Las Animas" just a few miles east. The Kansas Pacific road was trying to head off the Atchison, Topeka and Santa Fe which was then at Granada, sixty miles down, near the Colorado line.

On the north side near-by was old Fort Lyon, which still had a garrison of soldiers at that time, so here were three towns within a radius of a few miles. West Las Animas was a live hustling place, and soon absorbed the older town of that name. My brothers, George and Will, who had formed a partnership, were going to be shipping cattle from this point through the winter, so Brother George decided to rent a house and move into town in order to be at the loading point, and also to give Susie and me the advantage of the school. We were soon settled there. Living in town was a new experience for us, and a novel one that we enjoyed to the fullest. The school had only one teacher, a young woman from Kentucky, Miss Jennie Spooner. A fine girl with a commanding appearance, she managed her school in an efficient manner and gained the utmost respect of her pupils. She also taught music and here Susie and I had our first music lessons, given on the little organ that was moved down from the ranch; these lessons we enjoyed more than anything else.

The school was attended by several children of mixed breed, half- and quarter-breed Cheyenne Indians; bright, attractive children they were. Some of them were the children of the county judge whose name was Moore, his wife being a half-breed Cheyenne and niece of Charley Bent, one time governor of New Mexico. There were descendants of Kit Carson in the school, whether children or grandchildren I am not quite sure. They were part Mexican; Kit Carson's third and last wife was a Mexican, sister to Charley Bent's wife, and I believe these children were hers.

Some of our nearest neighbors here in Las Animas were John

Prowers and John Hough, brother of Si. They had a large commission house, did a big business, and were the leading citizens.
Prowers had fine ranches also, having acquired a lot of land
through his wife, a full-blood Cheyenne. They had several children and I think each child was allotted a section of land. He
was a splendid man and we liked him, for he was always affable
and pleasant to be with. Hough's wife was a sister of Prowers,
a fine dignified woman, superintendent of the Sunday school
and society leader. I imagine the Cheyenne sister-in-law, who
could not speak English, was somewhat of a cross to her, a real
thorn in the flesh, but this brother meant so much to them from
a financial standpoint, they could afford to countenance the
squaw. Anyway, they had to. Prowers treated his wife with the
utmost respect in public; I can remember only a few occasions
when they appeared in public together, once or twice at church
and once at a Christmas tree. She was always richly dressed
and a very kindly woman but not handsome by any means.
Many of the squaws I have known were rather handsome.

Susie and I visited in these homes and Mrs. Prowers was very
courteous. I remember one evening when we were in the Prowers
home with the Hough youngster and were trying a square dance,
Mrs. Prowers tried to show us some figures, but her English was
so limited she could not make us understand. One summer while
we were in Colorado, Father, Mother and I were driving through
the country and had dinner at Prowers' home ranch. Mrs. Prowers
did not sit down and eat with us, but served the meal even though
she had a cook whom she could have had help her. The dinner
was good and nicely served. After dinner she did not appear; I
think she was timid and felt her handicap in not being able to
speak English. I presume Mr. Prowers spoke Cheyenne to her all
the time and she had never bothered to learn his language.

While we were in Las Animas, Brother Will was in Chicago,

receiving and seeing to the selling of the cattle that were being shipped, a wonderful experience for him at his age. At the same time, Glenn and Phin were in St. Louis attending Jones Commercial College. This was an opportunity they could appreciate and they did good work, as they fully realized that this was more than likely their last school days. Phin led his class of three hundred boys in mathematics, which we thought was very praiseworthy. His older brother told this with pride when they came home, and now a younger sister tells it with pride, for his school days had been extremely limited and disconnected. This winter was the last school for any of us.

VI

This was a very cold winter even for Colorado, the mercury standing at thirty degrees below zero for many successive days. The Arkansas River was frozen and the cattle had to be crossed on the ice. The men had to haul loads of sand to sprinkle on the ice so that the cattle and horses would not slip down and break their legs or necks. What bitter weather it was! Those old cowboys would come in with ice over their faces where the breath had frozen to their mustaches. The cold did not stop them, though; they kept right on until the cattle were shipped out.

When we moved into town, Mother and Father went back to Point of Rocks where the houses were more comfortable and they would not be alone while we were away, for there were always some of the men on the ranch.

This winter my mother thought she would make a visit to her old home in Alabama that she had left so long ago. She was all ready, even to having her ticket bought, and was to leave early the next morning, but that night she could not sleep, so worried was she over the thought of leaving her family and making that long trip alone. The next morning she got up and announced

that she had decided not to go, turned her ticket in, and she and
Father drove back to the ranch. I am sorry now when I think
of her disappointment, for it really was a sore disappointment;
she needed someone to go with her. Her courage failed at the
thought of the long lonely trip, although in her young days she
had come out to a new frontier country alone so far as adult
company was concerned and had faced dangers and privations
of all kinds with never failing courage. Some years later she did
make the trip to Alabama alone.

As I look back on it now, this was a happy profitable winter
for the whole family. I know I enjoyed the school, the music
lessons, making new friends, and coming in contact with so many
more people, getting many things out of the book of life. I am
sure the winter was lonely for Mother and Father, but they were
happy to have us in school and could come to see us when the
weather was not too cold, as the ranch was only twenty-five miles
away. They spent Christmas with us, a notable one to me as I
saw my first Christmas tree. This will always stand out as the
most beautiful one I have ever seen. It was a tall spruce, fresh
from the Rockies, and reached from floor to ceiling of the church.
We had the privilege of helping to decorate it, stringing yards
of popcorn and cranberries, tying on apples and oranges. Still,
when it burst on my sight that night in all its glory of silver stars
and lighted candles, I gasped with delight, and have never seen
another quite so grand.

VII

The summer of 1875 saw the family reunited, Sister and Gus
having come out for a visit, and the boys all home again, Glenn
and Phin having worked their way in rather slowly. They came
over the Santa Fe which ended at Granada then, sixty miles from
Las Animas. At Granada they met up with some ranch outfit

and joined them, putting their trunk on the mess wagon. They had neither horses nor saddles, so they walked along with the wagon most of the time; they did not want to overload the team by riding in the wagon. At Las Animas they found the Reynolds cow outfit and were furnished horses and saddles. They came in looking a good bit like city dudes in spite of their long walk, for their faces were bleached from their winter indoors, and their white shirts, which the cowboys called "bald faced shirts," gave them quite a "city-fied" air.

Organ given to Sallie Reynolds by her father in 1875. Indian dolls in the shadow box were presented to her by Tonkawa Indians in 1869.

This summer brought me one of the most wonderful surprises of my life, one that gave me a great and lasting pleasure, a little cottage organ presented to me by my father. I do not believe a fortune dropped in my lap now could give me half the thrill that that plain, modest little Estey organ did then when it was landed at the door of our home. For years to come that organ was a source of pleasure; no grand piano was ever so sweet. I had learned enough about music in the winter to be able to study out simple pieces and by diligent practice I was able to make some progress. As for Susie, she was a natural musician and soon far outstripped me in that line. The organ is now in the home of a daughter, Ethel Matthews Casey, in San Antonio.*

Sister was having some dental work done this summer and had to go into town, Las Animas, several times. On one of these trips,

* In 1944 the organ was moved back to the B. W. Reynolds house in the Bend.

Susie and I were with her, and we were driving old "George," in single harness this time. We had to cross the end of a pond where he chose to sit down in a mud puddle. I cannot remember now how we managed to get him up; I do not think we got down in the mud, but the horse was surely covered with it. There was no man with us, just we three, but we got into Las Animas all right with our muddy horse. He was a fine gentle horse, would work in single or double harness, was gentle to ride, but he would sit down sometimes, although I never knew him to do it again; we brought him back to Texas with us and had him for years. His name was "George" when Father bought him from Mart Gentry who had brought him from California; we never would have given him that name as it was borne by one of the family.

Before going home, my sister went to Bristol, Connecticut, to visit the Bartholomew family. It was a bit out of the ordinary to visit the husband's family for the first time and leave him behind. The main motive was to place Gus, who was now ten years old, in school. His own father, being a native of Connecticut himself, had planned before his death to send him there when he was seven. They were very kindly received by the family and relatives. Sister said that one of the young cousins who came to see her seated herself on the sofa and gave her a critical looking over, then said, "Humph, I do not see but what Susan looks like the rest of the Yankees." I do not know what she thought she might look like; people in the East had some queer ideas about people from Texas. Several girls of the family went to the New England Conservatory in Boston at different times in later years, and they would be asked some funny questions. One, I remember, was how we got about down here, did we have any roads? They probably thought we were still blazing our way through forests with hatchets, and making trails.

Sister went home, leaving her little son in the home of Grand-
father Bartholomew. This required a brave spirit and a lot of
fortitude, for Connecticut was a long way from West Texas. He
stayed there five years without coming home but his mother
visited him every summer. On some of the visits, Brother Barney
went with her, but not every summer; although it was his home
and his people, he did not feel that they both could afford to go
every year. And like so many good, kind American husbands,
he gave the wife the trip to see her son while he stayed on the
job of providing a livelihood. There were never any more children
in this home, much to their disappointment. Brother Barney was
extremely fond of children and was adored by all the children
of the family.

When Sister came back after that first visit in Connecticut,
Susie was taken to Kansas City to meet her, going back to Texas
with her, so my friend and chum was gone, and I missed her
company greatly.

VIII

Now the Santa Fe system, not being the least bit bluffed by
the Kansas Pacific, had extended its road into Las Animas and
on up into our part of the country. Miles of it ran right along by
the side of the grade made by the Kansas Pacific. When the
Santa Fe reached Las Animas, there was a war to the finish;
freight rates were cut so low that people brought their cattle
from points a hundred miles away on the Santa Fe to take advantage of the low rates at this place. The Santa Fe won the
fight, and soon we were seeing the smoke and hearing the whistle
of the engines as they came up on the other side of the river. The
first railroad in a country is always something of extreme interest,
I think; I know this was to us. La Junta was established just

across the river from us, and the country seemed very prosperous.

Now, for some reason the family decided to quit this country and go back to Texas. My father's health had failed; the rigorous climate had affected him, at least that was what we thought, and he wanted to go back to Texas where the winters were not so severe. It may be they were all a bit homesick, I do not know. I thought little of that part of it at the time, I was too happy to be going back to Texas to be with my sister and childhood friends.

It seems a strange thing to me now, that my brothers should pick up and leave at a time when property values were certain to be going up, with a brand new railroad running right by them. We had a fine body of land all together, under a good irrigation system which was a worthwhile asset. And they had procured the land and houses so easily. I do not mean that life had been so easy for them, but they had gotten this land on easy terms from the Government, and it was just getting to be of some value. However it was, the decision was made and preparations were on for the move. It has been said that if our "foresight was as good as our hindsight," we might be better off from a financial standpoint. Be that as it may, this valuable property was sold for no fancy price, less than ten dollars an acre, and in a few years the same land sold for two hundred dollars an acre. I have no idea what it did get to be worth in after years, as the town of La Junta spread across the river and covers all that valley now. Such is life.

November, 1875, saw part of the family on the way to Texas. This time a car was chartered, and wagons, horses and furniture, and my little black dog that we called "Business" because he was such a busy little body, were loaded at Las Animas and started for Texas. A man by the name of Holstein came with the car to look after the livestock.

Glenn, being of an adventurous spirit, had gone with Hiram
Barber, our cousin, over into the mountains in the mining districts
of Colorado to try his fortune. Will and Phin stayed behind to
close out the cattle and wind up affairs on the ranch, while Ben
started down to Texas with a small bunch of Durham cattle.
These he left in the Panhandle of Texas in charge of Harry Milby,
a young man from Baltimore, who kept them there for the winter,
after which he brought them on down to the ranch which they
had made ready for them.

Kitchen, Barber Watkins Reynolds house, Reynolds Bend.

7   *Back to Texas*

I

Although the Missouri, Kansas and Texas Railroad had reached Sherman now, our car was unloaded at Denison for some reason. From there we drove to Merriman in Eastland County where Sister and Brother Barney lived. Here, Father, Mother and I spent part of the winter, while Brother George and Sister Bettie went on to the Matthews home near Fort Griffin. There was a pleasant surprise in store for me here; my school teacher, Miss Jennie Spooner, now Mrs. Will Vincenheller, was living in this little settlement of Merriman, her husband having a general merchandise store. It seemed strange that our lives should touch again so soon, and in Texas. I had heard nothing from her since our school days in Las Animas. Now I again had music lessons with her and was very happy.

While we were in Eastland County, Bennie had located a little ranch for my father and himself on the old Clear Fork, not so very far from the Stone Ranch where we had lived in the years gone by. He was having a comfortable stone house* built in a bend of the river, where it curved around at the foot of a rugged bluff on the north making a very attractive setting for a home. I was charmed with it when we came out later, and I think now that he used fine taste in the location of the house. The house was small without a suspicion of any architectural design, built

* Sketch opposite page 119.

in an "L" plan with living room, a combined kitchen and dining room, and a small bedroom on the lower floor. There were three bedrooms up-stairs, the stairway going up in the kitchen, and there were three fireplaces and one closet. We came out before it was finished and lived in a tent until the house was ready.

At last the family was permanently settled. Mattie Matthews, who had married Mart Hoover the year before, was living only a mile above us on the river where they had built a stone house, so we had a near neighbor already. This place was twelve miles above Fort Griffin which was still a flourishing garrison and the center of the social life. The Matthews family lived six miles below Fort Griffin and eighteen from us, but an eighteen mile ride on horseback meant nothing to us younger members of the family. We enjoyed that and were going back and forth quite often. While Fort Griffin was the social center, there were frequent house parties at both the Matthews and Reynolds ranches. There were fine pools of water in the river that made boating possible and this was indulged in to quite an extent. Croquet was a very popular game then and everyone had croquet grounds, this being our chief amusement. It has gone almost entirely out of date, being superseded by tennis and golf, but I still keep a croquet set for the grandchildren who are too young for tennis, and often the older ones join them in a game.

II

This year of 1875, the Indians were put on the reservation permanently after a concerted action from the different forts. General George P. Buell went out from Fort Griffin with a band of soldiers, others came out from Fort Sill to join them. General McKenzie was sent out from Fort Concho and I think to him is due the credit of settling them for good. These marauding bands of Indians had a way of slipping away from the reservation and making a raid down in Texas, then slipping back in without being found out by the agents. If they were questioned, they would appear very innocent. General McKenzie conceived the idea of setting them afoot; his theory was that if they did not have any horses they could not make these raids, as Texas was too far away for them to walk. Texas for some reason was especially hated by the Comanche and Kiowa tribes and they may have had just cause.

McKenzie got his troops ready and marched to the reservation, took their horses off and shot them. He killed fifteen hundred in one place west of here and that spot is called "McKenzie's Bone Yard." That was better than having a human bone yard as General Chivington did with the Cheyennes in Colorado. The road he made with his wagon train in going from Fort Concho to Fort Sill, Indian Territory, crosses the south side of what is our ranch today. When he was sent out from Fort Concho, he stopped at Fort Griffin several days waiting for supplies, and incidentally, the beef was furnished by Father Matthews. Texas was never raided any more after this; we were at peace so far as the Indians were concerned, but there were plenty of white men who did not mind depredating upon the country at large.

While on the subject of Indians, I want to quote a paragraph from a late book which has only recently come into my hands, nearly sixty years after McKenzie's Bone Yard was made. It is from the introduction by Hugh Latimer Burleson, Bishop of South Dakota, to *Facing the Future on Indian Missions*, a little book by Lewis Meriam and George W. G. Hinman.

Bishop Burleson says, "It is evidence of his sterling qualities of body and soul that the Indian has survived the successive stages of outright enmity, callous neglect and tardy recognition, that he has kept old friends and made new ones who see in him character values to be respected and developed. He is coming at last into his own in the land of his fathers where he has been too long a despised and despoiled alien. In this transition the government has a predominant part. To manly and generous officers of the Army who knew how to respect a gallant foe, and to pity helpless misery, to wise and kindly legislators, to humane and understanding officials of the Indian Service, to individuals and organizations that have fought his battles and demanded his rights, the Indian owes much."

Some may not think that this sentiment coincides with what was written before, but we do not judge all white men by a bunch of thieves and bandits, so why judge the Indian in that way? That has been done too much in the past. There are good Indians and bad Indians just as there are good and bad white men.

The year of 1875 was also the year the buffaloes were being exterminated and that was another strong factor in keeping the Indians on the reservation. Buffalo hunters went out with long guns that would kill at a great distance. They had trains of wagons and would load them with supplies for a winter's hunt, and in the spring hides would be corded by thousands in the side streets of the Flat. The scent of the hides would sometimes cause horses to stampede and run away with buggy or wagon.

We had two such runs, one when the team ran with an empty wagon and tore it to pieces, scattering it for miles. The other was by the same team, a pair of big sorrel horses; my brother George, was driving and was taking me and Georgia Spears to Camp Cooper from Father Matthews' place. Upon nearing Fort Griffin we came to a camp where they had buffalo hides and dogs. When the horses smelled the hides and heard the dogs bark, they snorted and away they went through the mesquites as hard as they could go, though Brother George was pulling on the reins with might and main, pushing with his foot on the dashboard until it was bent over. A back wheel came off and we were spilled out along the way but no one was seriously crippled and we came out of it very fortunately. That was the last time any one drove that team to a buggy; they belonged to Bud Matthews and he gave them to his uncle, William Spears, to put to a plow and keep them there.

Some writers have left the impression that these buffalo hunters who worked out from Fort Griffin were the scum of the earth. Some were but others were honorable and respected citizens. One of them, "Uncle" Joe McComb, is a fellow townsman of ours today and is as good a man as there is in town.

During the time the buffaloes were being slaughtered the Flat was at its zenith. There were enterprising merchants who carried first class merchandise, and a very good hotel, clean and well kept by Jack Swartz and his wife, served as headquarters for cattlemen. There was a school building which was also used for church services, with a Masonic hall on the second floor. Griffin had become a thriving place.

The Flat contained some who were as good citizens as one would find in any community. On the other hand it was teeming with wild and reckless characters of both sexes, adventurers, gamblers, desperadoes, horse thieves and cattle rustlers. Among this number was a woman gambler, a very mysterious person. She rented a cabin on the outskirts of town and established herself, and while she lived there no one was ever known to enter that abode except herself. She was known as Lottie Deno, "the poker queen" and was seldom seen except at the gambling table where she met famous gamblers, Monte Bill, Smoky Joe and others, and it is said that at the game of cards she was more than a match for the best of them. She had red hair, was a fairly good looking woman and was very intelligent. She was not at all afraid of doing the unconventional or unusual, and she illustrated this characteristic when she gave a masque ball one night at the same time another dance was on at the hotel. I have never heard of any reproach against her character other than her gambling, though she was shunned by the better class. However, she did not try to mix with them but kept entirely to herself.

One day she disappeared; no one knew where she had gone, who she was or whence she had come. Hoping to obtain some clue as to her identity or whereabouts, the sheriff and others entered her cabin and were astonished to find it handsomely furnished, at least it appeared so to those Westerners. Pinned to the bedspread was a note with these words: "Sell this outfit and give the money to some one in need of assistance." That was the last ever known of the mysterious Lottie Deno.

About this time, three brothers, cattlemen from Kansas and South Texas, came to our part of the country. With a large number of cattle and a big outfit, they started ranching on Miller and Lake creeks and on the Brazos River, trying to monopolize as much of the country as possible and to run things with a high hand, appropriating whatever they chose in range or cattle. However, they soon found that they had made a grave mistake, that they could not intimidate the old pioneers or crowd them out, so they began to calm down to some extent.

Then one evening the foreman of this outfit rode in to the Flat with one of his men and thought he would "paint the town red." He succeeded to a greater degree than he had bargained, for red blood flowed freely. He and two or three other men were killed outright, two of them, Lientenant Meyers, late of the Army, and Dan Barron, being innocent bystanders. A young lawyer, Jeffries, was shot almost to pieces but finally recovered. This was one of the most tragic affairs in the history of this wild western town and it put such a damper on the aforesaid ranchmen that they pulled up stakes and left the country, just as we were entering an era of peace and prosperity. Truly the way of the transgressor is hard.

During this period there was no law or order in the country, everyone being a law unto himself. The soldiers took no part in civilian troubles; it seems their business was to protect from Indians only, although the country was infested with bad men, some of whom were more dangerous than Indians. The best citizens decided it was time to do something so they banded themselves together to protect life and property. The times called for drastic measures and they were used to put down lawlessness of all kinds. The Vigilantes were on the alert and law and order were at last brought about.

III

We had been away from Fort Griffin only six years when we returned, yet it seemed a long, long time to me, at least twice that long. Our old friends, the Tonkawas, were still here. One day soon after we came back, Father, Mother and I were driving along the road from the Matthews Ranch to Fort Griffin, this being the first time we had come up from Eastland, when we saw an Indian at quite a distance from the road running toward us and frantically waving his arms to stop us. Father stopped the team and the Indian came up and greeted us enthusiastically.

My father said, "You do not know me."

"Yes! Yes!" the Indian replied.

"Well, what is my name?"

The Indian hung his head in thought for a moment, then pointed up the river and said, "You live up river. Got boy name George. Got boy name Will."

But still he could not call our name. Finally my father said, "Reynolds."

"Yes! Yes! 'Nullens!' 'Nullens!' "

This Indian whose name was Johnson had recognized my father from some distance and had come to greet him. When they were one's friend, they were loyal to the last. One of the most outstanding men of this small tribe and one who deserves special mention was named White, a keen old fellow who was not easily fooled in any way. He spoke English fairly well and I think he could speak Spanish too. He spent a lot of time in the Matthews home, often passing the day there. He liked to talk to Father Matthews and would often advance a very good thought. Once when he came to spend Sunday and found the family ready to go to church he was peeved and said, "Matthews, you heap scared, get good, go to church on Sunday. Tonkawa no scared, him good all time."

Another time when he was there, Bud jokingly told him to take something up to his squaw, indicating Miss Hall, the governess.

"Ugh!" said White in disgust. "She not your squaw, your squaw up river at 'Nullens.' " This was a well-founded observation as a later event will bear out.

Oftentimes when Father Matthews would be away from home, a number of these Tonkawas would come down to the ranch and pitch their tepees near the house. They had come "to keep the Comanches away from Caroline," they would say.

In these early days we had a very religious man in the country who had the habit of going out in the morning to some secluded spot for what he called "secret prayer." His prayer was not very secret as he seemed to think he had to talk in a very loud voice to be able to make the Lord hear him. One time he was visiting in Father Matthews' home, where there was a pack of hounds on the place. As was his custom the good brother walked off some distance through a corn field and began talking to the Lord in such loud tones that he aroused the dogs and they set up such a howl and yelping that the family thought Indians might be near.

Another time this pious soul went down into a little creek to pray. It so happened there was a little squad of Tonkawa Indians camped near-by and when they heard the noisy praying they stole up very quietly and peeped over the bank to see what it all meant. When they saw the man standing with his eyes closed and talking in a loud voice, they slipped away. Bud Matthews who was out after the horses happened along about that time and the Indians said, "Maybe so him too much." They thought he had had too much "firewater."

IV

Now comes another wedding in the family. Glenn who had returned from his expedition in the mining district, not having discovered any gold, was married on March 2nd, 1876, to Gustie Russell, and they located themselves for awhile at Point of Rocks which had not passed out of the family as yet. They still maintained the ranch while disposing of the remnant of cattle and Glenn fell into the ranch life again.

Father, Mother, Ben and I were now settled in the new home and enjoying it. One day I had ridden over to see Mattie Hoover when on my way home going along at an easy gallop, a fox ran across the road right in front of my pony and frightened him to such an extent that the little roan threw his ears forward and fairly flew over the ground. I was on a small flat sidesaddle with no girth, only a surcingle around it. The saddle soon came out from under the surcingle, and saddle and I fell to the ground together. The pony ran in home as hard as he could go with the bridle over head and the surcingle around his body. This of course frightened the very life out of my father and mother. Father jumped upon a pony that happened to be saddled near and came tearing up the road to pick up my broken body, while Mother, in tears, was following on foot. I had picked up my little saddle and was calmly footing it in, somewhat bruised, but not seriously hurt. I met them on the road and there was a fervent thanksgiving in their hearts right then to the Giver of all blessings.

This year the Matthews family had a governess, Miss Prudie Hall, for the two younger girls, Susie and Ella. She also taught music, both vocal and instrumental, and when I would visit them for a few days I would join in the studies and get a little benefit in this way. Every afternoon when school closed she would teach them voice, with "A's and Ah's," and have a regular sing-song. In the evenings we would sing while Miss Prudie played the organ. The songs would more often be hymns but there also would be some sentimental ballads and comic songs mixed in. We would dance and sometimes there would be young men for partners but often only girls. One would play the organ while the others waltzed, danced the schottische, the polka or most anything. We had a lot of fun and plenty of practice and good exercise.

If Fort Griffin with its Army group was the social center, the Matthews home was the center of hospitality. There was always something doing there and I somehow managed to be in the midst of most of it. They being near Fort Griffin saw more of Army life; we were twelve miles away on the outside border again and were not in as close touch with life at the fort as we had been in times past. The commandant of the fort at this time was Captain Irvine. The officers whom we had known in the past had long since been moved to other posts. Irvine followed General Buell who had been transferred after the Indian troubles were over. The Irvines were an elderly couple and while they were very pleasant, they did not get about as much as the younger

THE NATHAN L. BARTHOLOMEW HOUSE,
one of the family residences on the Clear Fork, built in 1876. Among the Eastern innovations which its New England-bred builder included was a kitchen sink, the first in Throckmorton County.

officers. I think Buell's term at the fort was the most brilliant from a social standpoint.

I believe Irvine's successor in command was Colonel Lincoln who had a lot of notoriety because he shot one of his own men, a negro soldier who had jostled him on the sidewalk. It was probably a mere accident but I suppose his pushing an officer was an act of insubordination, and very rude, and no Army officer could let a thing like that pass. Anyway, Lincoln whipped out his pistol and killed the man. The fellow was drunk most likely or he never would have been guilty of shoving against his commanding officer. Lincoln was tried in the civil courts at Albany, the new county seat of Shackelford County which had only recently been organized, and was cleared. He was then tried by court martial in San Antonio and acquitted. Father Matthews and Frank Conrad were called as witnesses for him in both courts. Some one asked Lincoln why he shot the negro. His reply was, "It was the only dignified course to pursue."

In the summer of 1876 Brother Barney sold his holdings in Eastland County and moved up near us, locating in the same bend of the river which we called Durham Bend because of a little herd of Durham cattle that we kept there. He began building a home, a larger and more commodious stone house and on a better plan than our little home although ours was on a solid foundation and still stands intact. The lumber for both these houses had to be hauled by wagon more than one hundred and fifty miles, the end of the Texas and Pacific railroad then being at Eagle Ford just west of Dallas.

The lime was burned at home and when Brother Barney had the wood laid and the stone piled on top of it ready to fire he went out early in the morning to start the kiln, followed by my little dog which had taken up with him and went everywhere with him. A few minutes after the fire was well under way they heard one little terrified yelp. Poor little "Business" had slipped into the kiln without being seen and was cremated. Brother Barney was distressed as he was very fond of the little dog and blamed himself for not taking care of him. We were all sorry because of the tragic end of the little pet.

This summer the Clear Fork overflowed all its banks and swept out into the valleys, something the oldest resident had never seen. The rain began on the 23rd of June, breaking up a big Masonic picnic that had been planned for the 24th at which they were going to have a public installation of officers. The Masonic fraternity was in great favor with the men at this time, there being a thriving lodge at Fort Griffin which held a meeting once a month in the light of the moon. Judge Stribling was the leading spirit in this organization.

My father had a farm in the valley near the river and at the time the flood came the corn was almost in roasting ear. The water came up so high that we could see only the tassels of the corn sticking up above the surface. The house was on higher ground and the water rose no higher than across the lower side of the back yard. The fall following the overflow of the river there was an unusually fine crop of pecans.

On the Fourth of July, this being the centennial of the Declaration of Independence, there was quite a celebration at Albany. This new town was situated about seventeen miles south of Fort Griffin. Susie, Bud, Bennie and I went over on the 3rd to attend the wedding of John Jacobs and Kate Graham. The Grahams were then living south of Albany at the old Ledbetter salt works where in earlier days Mr. Ledbetter who was now county judge had processed salt for the surrounding country. The wedding was at sunset, a very quiet one with only a few friends present.

There were several young people in the family and they had a platform built for dancing where we danced that night. We spent the night with the Graham family and the next day went back to Albany where quite a crowd had gathered for the Independence Day celebration. One of the things I remember was a tournament where the young men would run their horses by posts and take off rings with a spear, the one taking the most rings getting the prize. They had to run, not gallop. I enjoyed this immensely; it was the first tournament I had ever seen, having only read of them, and it savored of the sport of kings; one might easily imagine a spreading canopy with royalty seated beneath it watching the jousts of their knights, if one were very fanciful. Ed Manning, a rather new young man in the country at that time, took a prominent part in these jousts; he later married Molly, the daughter of Judge Lynch, one of the pioneers of the West.

That night there was a dance at the court-house, a temporary picket structure that did duty several years before being replaced by the present one of stone. There were only three or four houses in the place at that time, the court-house and the store of Colonel T. E. Jackson who was one of the pioneer merchants of the area; there was a sort of hotel where I think we had our meals that day and breakfast the next morning. There usually would be a barbecue and big dinner on such occasions but I cannot remember any barbecue that day which seems very strange. There were people there from all over the country and where they ate I do not know; I suppose they brought basket lunches. The young people stayed for a dance that night and kept it going until late. Around two o'clock in the morning a bunch of us girls were accommodated with shakedowns on the upper floor of Jackson's store. Who furnished these beds I do not know, but I do know they seemed very good to us and we were glad of the opportunity

of a few hours rest. I have an idea that Bud Matthews had this
room prepared for us as he took us over there.

The next day we went to the Matthews Ranch where Bennie
and I spent the night and drove on home from there. We always
seemed to have plenty of leisure time in those days; boys and
girls would visit and spend several days at the two homes. There
never was any great hurry to be going. Now we have every
convenience to make housekeeping easy and light, running water,
both hot and cold, gas and electricity, telephones with which
to order everything delivered to our doors, automobiles with
paved roads to run them over and if we are in a great hurry we
can take an airplane, yet we have so little time for visiting. We
rush, rush, rush here and rush there, and I do not see that we
accomplish an extraordinary amount. Do not think for a minute
that I am one who thinks the old times are best for I do not.
I think we are living in the "Golden Age" but I do wonder where
the time goes; it flies faster than a weaver's shuttle.

v

The summer of 1876 brings to me the most thrilling event
which comes into the life of any young girl, the entry of the
knight of her dreams. And who should my knight be but my
school-fellow and friend of childhood days, Bud Matthews, my
"Prince Charming" just the same. This was July and my lover
wanted to be married right away and take a wedding trip to the
Centennial Exposition then being held in Philadelphia. That was
entirely too hurried and I asked for a year. I was so young I
thought we should wait that long at least but like most young
lovers he insisted upon an earlier date, and being very persistent
he had his way. I did not seem able to resist him. Christmas Day
was his choice so that was the day set, about half of the year
asked for.

THE BARBER WATKINS REYNOLDS HOUSE,
built at Reynolds Bend on the Clear Fork in 1876. On Christmas Day of the same year Sallie Ann Reynolds married John Alexander Matthews in its parlor.

Now a trousseau had to be made ready. There were no dressmakers in this part of the country and "ready to wear" shops were unheard of in that day and time; we made our own clothes from start to finish. My sister who was an expert needlewoman came to the rescue with her *Bazaar* patterns. Brother Barney subscribed to all the Harper publications when they were first married and continued them for many years. She also had *Petersons Magazine*, another fashion book.

Sister Bettie and Brother George who were making one of their numerous excursions, on their way to the Centennial this time, sent material for the important dress. This was a white silk alpaca, half silk and half wool. In the early fall my father made a business trip to Weatherford and a cousin who lived near us, Ollie McLean, went along with him. We had her select materials and a hat, only one. There were stores at Fort Griffin that carried dry-goods but of course one had more from which to select in a larger place, although in later years Mr. Conrad carried an excellent line of goods and had an up-to-date store in every way.

Now we became very busy with the sewing. The wedding dress was made with a train, not very long, just medium, and had a wide pleated flounce around the bottom. There was a long tunic or overskirt as we called them then which was all tied up from the under side making it puff out in the back with a bouffant effect, and a little tight basque with lace on the bottom of it. I shall describe another dress as it was the so-called second day dress. It was of greyish tan, trimmed in blue buttons and blue collar and cuffs. It was made with a long Polonaise which had three rows of little blue buttons all the way from top to bottom in front and three rows on top of the sleeves from cuff to shoulder seam. The buttons were the common little rice shirt buttons and

I covered every one of them with the blue material. That was one of my jobs while Sister was doing the more important things such as cutting and fitting. It sounds queer and funny now perhaps but we were going by *Harper's Bazaar* and that was a standard authority on all questions of fashion. At that time the *Bazaar* had a fashion sheet with each issue and these patterns had to be traced out by lines of different design, some dotted, some dashed and some of other kinds. Sister had a tracing wheel with which we would work out these intricate pattern lines. Mine was a very simple little trousseau but I was perfectly satisfied and happy with it.

The family all came home this fall for the wedding. Brother Will and Phin came from Colorado as did Glenn with his young wife, Gustie, whom we learned to love dearly. This was a white Christmas and a very cold one. Snow began falling on the 20th of December and the ground was covered with several inches and frozen over. Ours was a small quiet wedding with only the two families, a few relatives who lived near and some special friends, among whom were Mart Gentry, John Pope and Lute McAbe. Susie Matthews was bridesmaid and George Kirkland, a young lawyer of Fort Griffin, best man. Judge Stribling said the ceremony, a very short one. We were married in the afternoon, that being most convenient as we were on the outside edge of the community and the Matthews family, who felt that they must go home, had a long drive. Another link in the chain which bound the two families was forged by this wedding.

Our one present except the household furnishings from our parents was a splendid new Miller buggy from Brother George. He could have given us nothing better or more useful. We did not take a wedding journey but we drove that buggy many miles during the winter, going back and forth between the two homes, spending a few days at each place.

The day after the wedding we used it to drive down to the Matthews home* over the squeaky frozen snow; a sleigh could have been used to advantage that day but this country knew nothing of sleighs and had little use for them. The buggy was mighty fine for riding over the snow. At the Matthews home we were royally entertained for this was the infare. The people from the surrounding country and the officers and their wives from the fort were there and there was the usual feasting and dancing, heralding a gay winter for us.

* Pictured opposite page 87.

Kitchen, Barber Watkins Reynolds house, with parlor beyond.

The California Ranch, built in 1877, was the house in which Sallie Reynolds Matthews did her first housekeeping as a bride. This sketch is based upon Mrs. Matthews's description of it.

8 *California Ranch*

I

ABOUT THE TIME we were married, Reynolds Brothers and Matthews had established a ranch together out in Haskell County, not as partners in business but simply running their cattle together, coöperatively. They built a crude stone house as stone was cheaper and easier to get than lumber. The house was not on any land owned by them; it was on a tract owned by Heber Stone of Brenham, Texas. It was the first ranch established in Haskell County, and this is where we started housekeeping. I was to be on the outside border again; it seems to have been my lot in life to be on the edge of things, not in busy centers. Nor do I look upon it as a bad lot, though most would think it very drab, but it may be that I do not know any better. At least, I am quite content and feel that "the lines have fallen unto me in pleasant places."

In the early spring of 1877, we packed into a wagon our few belongings consisting of my little organ, a Singer sewing machine, a bedstead with bedding and household linens which were given to us by the two mothers, two or three trunks, and a pair of pigs. We had a boy to drive the wagon and we started out in our buggy, following the wagon. The day was bright and balmy, but my heart was sad and heavy at leaving home for good. Up to now I had not realized what it meant to tear loose from Mother and

Father and make a separate home. I had been very light-hearted while we were running back and forth between the two homes, but *this,* this was different, and I could not keep the tears from flowing. The young husband was patient and sympathetic and my paroxysm of grief spent itself after awhile.

We crossed the Clear Fork two or three miles above my father's at Buzzard Peak, where the hill going down into the river was very steep, with hardly a road that could be seen. We made the crossing and started up a rugged canyon on the other side, Paint Canyon, deriving its name from Paint Creek which flows into the Clear Fork a short distance below its mouth. When about half way up the canyon, our wagon broke down and we had to send back to Father's for another wagon; the boy went back, riding one horse and leading the other; while we stayed with our belongings. He was gone quite a long time, and it was almost noon when the load was transferred from the broken wagon to the other, so we ate a lunch we had brought, then started on our way again. The road, which led over the steep rocky hills and canyons of the breaks of the Clear Fork, was rough and hard to travel.

Soon we came into the old California Trail, made by wagon trains that passed this way in the days of '49. It was only a dim trail now, but still marked with the ruts of wagon wheels which were plain enough for us to follow. Finally we came out from the rough breaks of the river into open prairie country where we could make some progress. The distance really was not very great, but it seemed to me we were getting to the jumping-off place; the road had seemed endless because of the roughness and the delay. After we left the roughs and thought it would be safe to leave the wagon, we drove on to the ranch, arriving there at dark, having driven less than twenty miles. After our first visit back home, the road never seemed so long and lonely any more, as familiarity always seems to lessen distances.

Finding one's self in a strange place in the dark is not very inspiring, but Brother George and Sister Bettie were there ahead of us, they having come from the Matthews home over the McKenzie Trail from Fort Griffin; they had a newer and better road, though a much longer one, that did not come through the rough country that we did. My spirits revived considerably on finding them there. The ranch house looked like an old stage stand, it was so long, having four rooms all in a row, with three fireplaces. The cowboys had the east room with fireplace, the kitchen came next, then our room, with Brother and Sister in the west room. There was a stack chimney between these two rooms, making a fireplace in each. It was a comfortable house, the thick stone walls keeping out both heat and cold. Every room had an outside door on the south. The doors were not all up when we reached there that night, and the boys had nailed boards across some of them to keep the calves out.

Here we set up housekeeping, and having Sister Bettie there with me during the first few months of it was a great comfort. She was leader, and it was almost like being with Mother, although I felt that I must take my share of the responsibilities. Then she and Brother often traveled about, so were not there very much, and during those times I would have all the work to manage, but the cowboys were considerate and helpful. I never had to bring in a stick of wood or bucket of water. They would grind coffee and slice the meat, and do many other things to help. We had to roast our own coffee in those days, and one time when I had a large batch in the stove roasting, I let it burn black. I was so humiliated and ashamed that I took it out and buried it so that no one would know how careless I had been.

This was called California Ranch because the house was on California Creek, so named because the old trail ran along beside it almost to its source. Most of the creeks were named in a similar manner, that is, because of some circumstance connected with a particular creek. There is one called Dead Man because in an early day a man was found dead on it. There is a Tin Cup Valley, so styled for the reason that some one once found a tin cup there. The creek which flows into the Clear Fork immediately above the site of old Fort Griffin is Collins because a man of that name was hanged on its banks long ago, and the one next below is Mill Creek because the old saw-mill established by the fort was located near, and it bears that name to this day. If a creek was not named in such a way, it usually derived its name from some outstanding characteristic. Such were Boggy and Rocky, the names of which are self-explanatory, and Paint, so-called because its water, colored by the soil through which it flows, is a vivid red when there is a freshet, and colors the Clear Fork where it runs in.

As I have said, there was no other ranch in the county, so we had everything our own way, "monarchs" of the whole county range, and it was a grand one for ranching. The boys built another little house of stone, just a line camp over on North Paint, a tributary of the main Paint Creek that came in on the north, and was ten or twelve miles north of where we were. In the summer, Sister Bettie and I went over and spent a few days while the branding was going on. We had very good fishing and occupied our time tramping up and down the creek with a fishing pole every day, keeping them supplied with fish.

One time when the men were working the cattle at this place and had a large herd in the pens all settled for the night, so they thought, a meteor came down and burst so near that they could hear a hissing noise. The cattle stampeded and broke the pens, scattering in all directions. As a result of the untimely advent of the meteor, all the hard work had to be done over.

Rice Derrett, one of the cowboys, when riding the west side of the ranch one day, discovered a fine spring of water which was sufficient for watering many cattle at one time. This was a lucky strike and a great asset. The spring was promptly named "Rice's Spring" and when the county became settled and organized, the county seat was located there and called Rice's Spring until it was found that there was another post office of a similar name that caused mail to go wrong. The name was then changed to Haskell.

Brother George and Sister Bettie were not with us many months, only the first few, as they began building a home on the river near my father's. It was across the river on the north side, but west of my father's as the river made a horseshoe curve to the south here. They built a stone house* on the same plan as Brother Barney's. It took a few months to build these houses and get them ready for occupancy. Stone was plentiful and near, but stone masons were not very efficient, neither were the carpenters. However, we did have a first class painter and his work withstood the ravages of time. Notwithstanding any crudenesses, the houses were comfortable and liveable, far better than the ones of earlier days; they seemed splendid to us.

When Brother and Sister left, Glenn and Gustie came, with their baby, Elmer Glenn, and took their place on the ranch with us, so we were not alone. Then there were always from four to six cowboys and sometimes more. The regular ones at that time were Tobe Butler and John Matthews, both cousins of the Matthews, John White, Will Howsley and Rice Derrett, all fine young men, and there were line riders scattered about in different camps who would be dropping in often. We were all one big-sized family and have known nothing else.

* Sketch opposite page 143.

All the boys liked to gather around the little organ in the evening and sing. Glenn, John White, who sang bass, and Tobe all had good voices, and Bud had a fine ear for music. Tobe could read music and carry any part, soprano, tenor or bass, and Gustie sang alto. We had a copy or two of *Gospel Hymns*, and everybody would join in; many of our evenings were spent in that way.

One time while we were on this ranch, our old-time pioneer Baptist preacher, Mr. Slaughter, came to see us, and that evening we had a preaching service; he had a fair sized room full, too. We also had a Methodist "circuit rider" to visit us, Uncle Jimmie Jones, accompanied by his wife. These itinerant preachers sent out by the Methodist Church were coming into the country now, visiting the scattered ranches.

As said before, in that day the ranch business was very different from the present. There were no fences, everything was open range, and some of the cattle would wander away in spite of line riders, or anything we could do. In the spring there would be a general round-up of each rancher's special range, and every ranchman would send one or two, usually two, men to these round-ups to represent his interests, and sometimes there would be as many as seventy-five or a hundred men, perhaps more, at one of the general round-ups if a large range.

This annual round-up in the spring was the event of the year and was really an interesting and spectacular affair. Imagine several thousand cattle brought together on the open prairie with rolling hills for a background, men weaving in and out of the vast herd, each separating his brand. This was called "cutting" and there were horses called "cutting horses" trained to this special work. Some of them would show great intelligence; when once an animal was started, the horse would keep right after that one until it was driven out of the herd, with very little direction from the rider. Then the second man would take charge and drive the cattle that had been cut out to one side and keep them together, "holding the cut."

The man whose range it was would have his mess wagon and cook, perhaps two cooks, and would furnish the dinner for all when they came together. They would butcher a beef and there would be one or two camp kettles of beans. The kettles were of sheet iron with a bail and held five gallons. There would be great pots of coffee, ribs broiling on spits before the fire, and the bread would be fresh baked in Dutch ovens. An expert cook would have a few flat round cakes of bread ready when the men came in to dinner, and with two or three ovens he would turn the bread out, hot and well cooked, as fast as the men could eat it. It was "sour dough" bread, made by first beating up a batter of flour and water and allowing that to ferment, to be used later with soda, salt and lard. The dough was mixed with that leaven and each time biscuits were made, some of the sour dough would be left in the vessel and more flour and water added to it; that kept it going. We had a man, Billy Peak, who was a marvel at cooking sour dough bread; he would pat a thin cake out in the oven, put a hot lid over it and in a jiffy it would be ready to eat, and it tasted good, too. Every man served himself from pots and kettles, and all sat down on the grass to eat.

Sometimes the ranch women would get together and plan a surprise for the boys. We would cook up a lot of nice things and go out and have dinner with them, making a gala day of it. We enjoyed seeing the extensive herds of cattle.

Each man would drive his cut back to his own range. In the winter time the cattle would drift south from the cold northers, at times going almost to the border of Mexico. From here an outfit of men would be sent to gather them in, sometimes being away a month.

II

In the early fall, I went home to Mother, and on the 21st of November our little Annie Caroline, named for her two grandmothers, was born. She was a wonderful baby, with violet eyes which changed in a few months to very dark brown, almost black. Oh, how proud I was of those dark eyes!

This same fall, a nephew of my mother's, David Campbell, from Wetumpka, Alabama, came out and joined the family. A younger brother had made a short visit here a few months before, and these were the first relatives of my mother that she had seen since leaving Alabama more than thirty years before. David had been in Texas for some time; he came here from Houston and was soon joined by his wife, Myra Benson, and their little daughter. They spent some time in my father's home, then went to Brother Barney's where they stayed until their home was ready for them, another little stone house just across the river on the north at the mouth of Ranger Creek. We found these cousins very agreeable additions to our family circle, and they have been associated with us all these years since.

After spending the winter at home, we all went back to the little ranch house in Haskell County where we were still the only ranchers in the county. But others soon began coming to this wide domain of public land. Texas, unlike the other states, owns all the public land in the state, none of it ever having been owned by the United States Government. We could not expect to use a whole big county very long and we began to have neighbors. Jim Reed brought a herd of cattle and located them not a great ways west of us, with a young man named Merrill in charge of them.

A few years later, Tom Merrill had a sad fate. He had married a young woman in Hot Springs, Arkansas, moved his cattle down on the border of Mexico and located a ranch on the Rio Grande.

One Christmas time he had let all his men off for a holiday, having only one Mexican man on the place. That evening he and his wife were murdered while at the supper table. When found he was sitting at the table, leaning over it with his head severed from the body. Evidently he had been killed first while his wife tried to escape, but her body was found near-by. The house was robbed of all valuables and the murderer or murderers escaped across the Rio Grande and nothing more was known of them. It was thought the murder was committed by the man on the ranch as he had disappeared, but that was conjecture. This was a ghastly find for the neighbor who happened in later.

On March 19th, 1878, a baby was born on the California Ranch, a little son, Ashel Watkins, to Gustie and Glenn. Neither doctor nor nurse was present, only Glenn and I to take care of the mother and new-born baby, while Bud took charge of the other two children. We had had a practical nurse and midwife out for days beforehand, our old negro mammy, Aunt 'Melia, who had belonged to our grandmother back East and had nursed us; but she was called to a daughter in the same trouble and assured us that she would be back in time to take care of this case, arguing that we expected it too soon. Nevertheless, the night after she left, the baby was born and we had to face the situation with all the courage at our command. Everything went well; our Heavenly Father takes care of his foolish children. We were very unwise not to have made some other provision. One thing I had done, however, was to have Aunt 'Melia give me all kinds of instruction and advice as to what to do in case of an emergency. We were all so young and inexperienced; I was not yet eighteen. As I look back upon it now, I wonder how we lived through it all. The next morning Glenn went after my mother and Cousin Sallie Reynolds, a niece of my father's who had come to make her home with my parents. How glad I was to see them!

The responsibility of the world rolled off my shoulders when they arrived.

Not long after this, I had another trying experience. Some people had come in with a little bunch of cattle and camped a few miles above us on the creek. They had been there only a few days and I did not even know that there was a family near, but I presume the men knew about them. There was a young man with his wife and baby girl about a year old, the wife's brother and others. One morning before day, some one called, "Hello! Hello!" waking us up; it was the young brother. His sister was very sick and they wanted help. They were utter strangers but they were in trouble, so my little bay mare, "Gritty," was saddled, and I mounted, feeling very efficient, I suppose, with a "heart for any fate," and set out at a gallop with this stranger in the dark. We arrived at the camp as daylight was coming; it was early fall and there was a chill in the air. The poor woman was lying there in the tent in a most pitiable condition. There had been a miscarriage and it was very evident that she was in the last stages of tuberculosis. Well, I did have sense enough to know that I could not cope with this; I needed help, so a man was sent across into the next county to the nearest ranch, some ten or twelve miles away, while I did what I could for the sick woman. Early in the day the man was back, bringing Mrs. Kiggins and Aunt Nancy Pate, and what a relief it was to see these kind, motherly women. Uncle Jessie Pate, brother of these two women, came to Texas with the Matthews family.

A man was sent to Fort Griffin for Dr. Baird and when he came he said the woman must be taken into a house. Ours being the only one near, I told them to bring her there. It was getting late now and I went home, tired in body and soul. In the meantime Gustie had taken care of my baby who was less than a year old and still nursing. I prepared my room and bed and they brought the sick woman down and put her in it, while we had a shake-down on the kitchen floor. We kept her and the baby a month, Gustie and I taking care of her. We had a cook, a man, who also helped us with the laundry. When we got her on her feet and she could walk about a little, they took her back to the camp for awhile, then moved her to Fort Griffin where she lasted only a few weeks before dying.

While this invalid was with us, I developed malaria from some cause, mosquito bite, I suppose, or this woman may have had the germ in her system. As I have said, we knew nothing then of the malaria germ or of the mosquito communicating the disease. Neither did we know that tuberculosis was contagious or infectious or we would not have been quite so reckless of the health of our families. I had chills and fever, and would almost shake my teeth out with an ague which would be followed by a high fever. These would come every other day with consistent regularity until I could get my system saturated with quinine; then I would have three weeks rest when they would begin again if I did not resume dosing myself with quinine.

In the spring of 1878, there was a fine crop of wild plums and we wanted to preserve some. We had no self sealing jars or any other jars for fruit on this ranch, but that did not stop us. We had a fifteen gallon molasses keg which was empty, so while the boys would gather the plums, Gustie and I would cook them in sugar, making a very nice preserve. We filled this keg, covered it and set it away for winter use in a little storehouse. This was the first part of June. Then we went home for a visit which lasted until early fall. When we returned to the ranch, there was a small bowl of preserves on the table, the last of fifteen gallons; the boys said that they were beginning to ferment so they just ate them. We had a bit of fun over this for the preserves very likely did ferment.

Another incident of this absence was a broken bottle. I had a very nice silver castor, or cruet stand (now long gone out of date), with etched bottles, my first Christmas present from Bud after we were married. The first thing after I came home, I noticed among the bottles an odd one. When I asked one of the boys, John Matthews, about it, he threw back his head and laughed as if it were a great joke and said, "We did not think you would ever notice the change; a chicken got on the table and one of the boys threw a stick of stove wood at it and broke the bottle." The mystery to me now is where they found that vinegar cruet, for we were so isolated on that ranch. I never thought to ask then or afterward while he was alive. Some of the boys must have found it at Fort Griffin.

Now Haskell County began to be occupied by actual settlers; people began to buy land. Some of it was already owned by individuals but they were all non-residents like Heber Stone of Brenham; the cattlemen did not hesitate to use these unoccupied lands, and even built houses on them, as we did. We still had no families near us, just a scattering of ranches. There were plenty of men moving about, but we were yet the only women in the county.

One time while living at the California Ranch, we sent John White to Weatherford for supplies. We could get groceries at Fort Griffin, but we usually bought our supplies from wholesale houses as we could buy them more cheaply. We would get sugar by the barrel, bacon by the five hundred pound case, and now that we could get canned goods we bought that by the case, tomatoes, corn and peaches, with fifty pound sacks of dry beans and apples, and one to two thousand pounds of flour. White loaded his wagon too heavily and had a hard time getting home; his team would be stalled at the hills and he would have to take part of his load off and carry it up. He was two or three days overdue and we had one meal, I remember, of nothing but corn bread. We could have killed a beef, but we did not for it was late winter when cattle were not fat enough to kill. In those days we did not have much milk and butter in the winter because of the scarcity of feed stuff. White came in that afternoon, and the next morning a man who lived over on the Clear Fork brought us a fine wild turkey, all nicely dressed, so we had a real thanksgiving dinner that day.

In later years John White, having saved some money, decided he would buy some cattle and put them on the range with ours. He rode horseback down into Palo Pinto County and there contracted for some cattle with a man named Gordon. For some reason Gordon refused to accept a check, so White rode all the way back to Albany to get the money. There was no bank in Albany at that time but F. E. Conrad was in the mercantile business there and he cashed his check for twenty-one hundred dollars. He rode off with all that cash in his pockets and that was the last ever seen of John White.

When he did not return on time, we became anxious and feared foul play, so Arthur Jeffries, who was with us on the ranch, started out to hunt for the lost man. When he got down to Palo Pinto County he found the horse headed toward home and the saddle with all equipment lying in the corner of a field just as though White had thrown it there and left it. All the circumstances indicated that White had been made away with. A private detective was employed and put on the case but not a trace of the missing man was ever discovered although we had our suspicions. The mystery of John White's disappearance has never been solved.

Another man mysteriously vanished while we were at California Ranch and Gustie and I were the last to see him in this part of the country. The circumstances of this case were very peculiar and tragic, tragic because of the shadow cast upon the life of an innocent man.

In the early 'Seventies a man named Brock came to Fort Griffin from the North, Ohio or Indiana. He was a strange sort of person, extremely reticent and not at all friendly, the kind of personality that was out of place on the western frontier and because of his peculiar nature he was shunned by most of the people. He worked in the sutler's store but before long he had started a little side line which eventually grew into a profitable business.

At this time huge trail herds were constantly coming through from South Texas headed for the North and they, together with the buffalo hunters, made a thriving business for Griffin. In these trail herds there were always a number of "drags," young calves and cattle too weak to keep up with the herd. The men in charge of the herds would sell the drags for very little or in some cases might even give them away. Brock got his start by picking up the drags as the herds came through Fort Griffin and it was not long until he had accumulated a little herd of cattle. He located a ranch on Foyle Creek and sent back North for two cousins, Ed and Frank Woosley, to help him run the ranch. He practically turned it over to them but I do not think they owned any interest in it.

One morning Frank Woosley came to the California Ranch hunting our cow outfit, and I told him where I thought he would be able to find them. He got down off his horse, adjusted his saddle, mounted again and rode away. That was the last ever seen of him in West Texas.

For some reason people got it into their heads that Brock had made away with Woosley and the vigilance committee came very near hanging him, but he protested his innocence and as the evidence against him was meager and circumstantial, nothing was done to him. This did not close the case for Brock because he was determined to vindicate himself as there were many who still thought he was guilty. He quit everything to commence a long search for Woosley. His body had never been found and Brock was confident that he was alive. He would follow every clue, traveling from state to state, and often would be gone for long periods of time. It is said that his hunt extended not only over the United States but into Canada and Mexico as well. When he had spent everything he had, he again went to work but only long enough to acquire sufficient funds with which to resume his search. He would repeat this procedure whenever he found himself without resources. Finding the missing man was always uppermost in his mind, it was all he was living for, it had become an obsession. People would avoid him as much as possible for while others were forgetting the case he could talk of nothing else.

Years passed and Brock's search for his kinsman seemed hopeless but he did not give up. After long and fruitless seeking he received a letter from a man down in Arkansas, somewhere near Hot Springs, telling him that he thought he had found his man. With renewed hope Brock set out at once for Arkansas, getting off the train at a little station called Bald Knob, but upon seeing the man in question, he said, "No, he isn't Woosley." This clue like all the others he had followed had proved to be false, and disappointed and disheartened, he returned to the railroad station. He walked up to the ticket window to buy his ticket home and there he stood face to face with his man.

Frank Woosley had married and was living there under an assumed name. Brock took him in charge and returned with him to their old home in Ohio or Indiana to have him publicly identified. In the meantime Ed Woosley who had been in ill health had died. The Woosleys' plan probably had been to have Frank vanish mysteriously, then to sow the seeds of suspicion against Brock among the people of the community, as was done, with the idea of his being hanged by the vigilance committee. In this way Ed would acquire Brock's property and after a period of time Frank might return with some plausible story as to his absence and share the ranch with Ed. If the plot was such, it fell through when the vigilance committee decided not to hang Brock, but whatever it may have been, it wrecked the life of an innocent man.

The Tecumseh Ranch House was destroyed by a cyclone after Sallie Reynolds Matthews and her husband had moved from it. This drawing is based upon Mrs. Matthews's description of it.

9 *Tecumseh Ranch*

I

AFTER A TIME Glenn decided to enter the sheep business, and moved down on the Clear Fork, establishing a small ranch a short distance above old Camp Cooper where he built a little stone house. After Gustie and Glenn left, the ranch was rather lonely for me as the men would be out all day, although I was getting somewhat seasoned. Howbeit, we decided to turn the ranch over to the cowboys to run, and to go where there were more people and where we could get a little more in touch with the world. Soon we bought a small ranch located on Tecumseh Creek which comes into the Clear Fork from the north about eight miles above Fort Griffin. This place was on the old Comanche Indian reservation which was a body of land six miles square. On this land old Camp Cooper had been built to keep a check on the Indians and to try in a way to civilize them by teaching them agriculture. The Indians were not hostile while on the reservation; it was after they were moved into the Indian Territory that they became so bitter. They may have resented being taken away and may have held that against Texas. It is true that they depredated to some extent while here for it was during this time that Cynthia Ann Parker was taken but they were not so venomous as they became later. I shall not tell the story of Cynthia Ann, the little white

139

girl who was captured and later married to an Indian chief, as that can be found in other sources.

There are, however, other incidents that occurred among our friends and neighbors. One of the most atrocious cruelties was the scalping alive of a little twelve year old boy, son of Mr. T. E. Jackson. The little fellow had walked out a short distance from the house to drive the calves in at the evening milking time. A band of Indians ran onto him, knocking him down with their horses; then one dismounted and quickly tore the scalp from the crown of his head, at which they ran away doubtless thinking the child dead. The little boy got up, picked up his hat and calf whip, and walked home. His mother, probably paralyzed by fright, heard every cry but was powerless to help. I am persuaded that there were mothers in the country who would have grabbed a weapon of some kind and have gone to the rescue of their children. He lived only a few months more, dying as a result of the wound.

Another incident was the taking of John Ledbetter, seven year old son of Mr. Ledbetter who became the first county judge of Shackelford County. Ledbetter was living at the old salt works at the time, where he had been used to skirmishes with Indians. John was staying with the Lynch family and going to school. Mr. Lynch, ever an up-to-date citizen, having hired a teacher for his own children, took in other children to give them the benefit of the school which was taught in his home. One day at the noon hour John failed to come back in for lessons. He had vanished. The people were notified and the whole country turned out en masse to look for him. Mr. Lynch was away from home at the time and it is said that he swam swollen streams in order to get back and join in the search. I heard Mr. Ledbetter say that there was not a dead rabbit in the country but what was found, but there was no trace of the missing boy.

Some eight or ten years after, while we were living here at the Tecumseh place, a young man appeared in Griffin. He was dressed in a sort of semi-Indian garb and had the appearance of having grown up in the wilds. Some of the older citizens became interested and thought it possible from his remarks that he might be the missing boy, so they sent for Judge and Mrs. Ledbetter. They came and after questioning him for awhile they began to believe that he was their lost boy though he did not seem to recall anything about his early life. They took the boy home with them and told him that if he was their son he had certain marks on his body, a birthmark and some scars from burns. When the children were young they would play at branding cattle; one day they had some hot irons and really branded this boy. On examination it developed that he had the marks on his body just as Mrs. Ledbetter said and she and Mr. Ledbetter were firmly convinced that he was their lost child. The boy, however, was not so certain. Although he stayed with them quite a while and after leaving them would come back for an occasional visit, he finally repudiated the family entirely and now goes by the name of "John Wesley."

After the Indians were moved, this land came back to the State and was open for preemption in one hundred and sixty acre tracts. The only requirements were that a man must have a wife and actually live on the land a certain length of time; three years, I think, was the time required; then he could get a patent and acquire title. He had to pay something to get a patent and that was all the cash he would be out. In consequence of such easy terms this land in and around Camp Cooper was pretty well occupied, making a fair sized neighborhood, six miles each way. The place which we bought was on this reservation and was called "The Tecumseh Ranch" and still goes by that name. The first house was destroyed by a cyclone some years after we left it. The ranch is now owned by Reynolds Cattle Co.

There was a good, well built stone house there of three large rooms. The plan of the house was an "L"; that seems to have been a favorite plan, a very good one, too. It was unfinished, having no paint or plaster. We added a porch on the front and in the "L," had cupboards and wardrobe built in and had the house painted and plastered inside and out. When we had the outside stucco painted grey and penciled in white we thought we were doing something extra nice. We had first class workmen on this house and all the work was well done. We lived in the house several months before having it worked over.

When we first set up housekeeping we subscribed to two publications, the *New York Weekly Sun* and *Demorest Magazine,* a fashion book and all round household magazine. I especially enjoyed regular stories by "Jennie June," Mrs. David Goodman Croly, founder of "Sorosis," the first woman's club in the United States. These publications were of lasting benefit to us, I am sure, keeping us somewhat in touch with what was going on in the big world, so much bigger then than now so far as coming in contact with people and things is concerned. Now we touch elbows with all nations.

This winter of 1878 there was another wedding on foot in the family and we went down to Father Matthews' to help with the preparations. All through Christmas week the cooking was being done; cake, cake, cake, I never saw so many or such enticing ones. A young lady late from Kentucky with whom we had become acquainted, Sadie Vincenheller, came for a visit and stayed to help. She was a past master in the art of making and decorating cakes and she certainly was an asset at that moment. There were seventy-five chickens killed beside other meats, turkey and boiled hams, and there were pies by the dozen. I wonder now how in the world all this cooking was done; some of it was done on a

THE GEORGE T. REYNOLDS HOUSE,
built in 1877, was the last of the family residences constructed of stone on the Clear Fork. It was the home of "Brother George and Sister Bettie."

fire out of doors. Mother Matthews was a wonderful manager and had a lot of helpers, white and black. It took a manager to keep all that crew at work but she was always in the lead, up at the break of dawn and going late.

The trousseau was made by a French dressmaker who had been discovered in Fort Worth, Mrs. C. D. Brown, whom many of the older generation will remember. The wedding dress was a white swiss and the dress for the next day was wine colored silk. Anything that Mrs. Brown made had the "Magic touch" for she was an artist in her line.

On the first day of January, 1879, all was ready. A partition had been removed from between the two front rooms to make a large room for dancing. Long tables were set in the yard all covered with white linen and decorated with evergreen vines, a few red berries and mistletoe full of white waxy berries. There was very little in the way of green things at this season but we utilized what we had. The afternoon was bright and sunny, not too cold. At two o'clock Brother Will and Susie Matthews stepped out on the front porch and facing a yard full of people were married. Judge Stribling officiated, Mary Spears, a cousin of the bride, was her maid, and Nick Eaton, a cattleman, was best man. In the evening there was dancing which continued all night with plenty of refreshments in the way of cake and coffee at all times. A lot of people went home but there was a house full left and they were there for breakfast the next morning.

On the day after the wedding, the 2nd of January, there was a cold norther blowing and the crowd that was left faced that norther for eighteen miles up to the home of Brother George and Sister Bettie where an infare was held. This was a repetition of the day before, only the crowd was not so large, not so many invitations having been issued. Father Matthews, lovingly called "Uncle Joe" by the whole country, would invite everybody in the surrounding area to a wedding in his home; he could not bear to leave out any one he knew and he knew everyone. This wedding made another link in the chain binding the two families together.

The young couple went to Galveston on their wedding journey. When they returned they lived in the home of Brother George and Sister Bettie until they built one of their own in this family neighborhood. William's gift to his bride was a splendid piano, an old-fashioned square one. They, like many other things of that time, have passed out. This was the first piano brought to Throckmorton County and my little organ was the first keyboard instrument in the county.

II

After all the wedding festivities were over we settled down again into the routine of living. In the spring we improved our house, planted our orchard and garden and a few flowers and vines. One wild grape planted at the west end of the front porch ran across the end and front making a garland all around the porch in later years. The "L" porch when covered with morning glories made a pleasant summer dining room.

Now we were living in a community where there was a school, and preaching services once a month, sometimes oftener. This community had a number of Primitive Baptists, "Hard Shells" they were called, so most of our preachers were from that sect although there would be Methodists or Missionary Baptists part of the time. We always attended these services. Often there would be three of the Primitive preachers and each one would preach. One day one of them seemed to be getting on in a good way when he suddenly said, "My light has gone out," and sat down. Even a Primitive could be temperamental at times.

While this was only a country school taught in a little log room, the teacher, Professor Dalrymple, was an unusually fine one of that day and time. Many of the younger generation look back upon his regime with pleasant memories. That little community was very fortunate in securing such a fine cultured man for a teacher; his was an influence for good in the country. There were a few people with vision and ambition for their children, among them Uncle William Spears, brother of Mother Matthews, who was living at Camp Cooper at this time and had several children of school age. He was one who wielded an influence in behalf of good schools. Ella, my young sister-in-law, a girl in her teens, attended this school from our home. John Matthews, a cousin, was with us and went to school, and added to these, we had taken an orphan boy, Henry, a young brother of John Labrier who was on the ranch, so we as usual had a fair sized family.

This spring of 1879, there were wedding preparations on again for another Reynolds-Matthews union. This time it was my brother, Ben, and Florence Matthews, a niece of Father Matthews, who had come out a few months before from Arkansas and was spending some time with Brother George and Sister Bettie. The result of this visit was a wedding which was celebrated in that home on May 6, 1879, in the usual manner. The bridesmaid was Ella Matthews, and F. E. Conrad who at that time was beginning to pay court to Ella, was best man.

The infare was held at my father's home. I came over from Tecumseh some days beforehand to help Mother get ready for it. Henry Labrier, a boy of thirteen, was driving the team, a pair of mules, and a young girl who helped me with the housework and baby was along. We were crossing Ranger Creek, fording it end ways we would say, but the road was so dim we missed it and came upon a steep place. We saw that we were wrong but could not stop the mules; they went right over the bluff and dumped us into a pool of water and calmly stopped. For-

tunately the water was not deep and none of us was hurt. We
scrambled out and walked down to Cousin Dave Campbell's,
near by, where we got into some dry clothes while he went back
and helped the boy right the buggy which was lying on its side
in the pool of water. They soon had it right side up and we went
on across the river to Father's, only a short distance.

Myra would come over every day and help with the preparations and she was a most efficient helper, too. We always had a
lot of fun getting ready for these affairs even though it was work.
Myra was just out from "the States" so could give us some dots
and we were ever ready for new ideas. She made delicious lemon
pies; they were new things to us then.

III

February 14, 1880, a little son was born to Susie and William
and was named George Eaton. On the 14th of May our home was
blessed with another little daughter, Mary Louise, named for
her Aunt Mary and a friend, Louise Conrad, sister of F. E. Soon
after these important events my mother had her first visit to her
old home in Alabama after an absence of thirty-three years.
Myra Campbell was going home to visit her family, and Mother
went with her. After such a long absence there were many
changes in Mother's family; some had died and many new ones
had been born. There were still two brothers, a sister and one
sister-in-law living, one of the brothers being the eldest, David
C. Campbell. She stayed for some time, enjoying these brothers
and sisters and having a pleasant visit, then came home alone,
leaving Myra who returned several months later bringing a new
baby girl, Reubie.

This summer several others of the family took a trip. The men
were taking cattle to Fort Worth to ship to market. John (I had

to stop calling him "Bud" as that was not a very dignified name for a wife to call her husband, so I learned to say "John" though I had called him "Bud" from the time I could lisp) had charge of the herd and went that far with it. Mother Matthews, Ella, Sister Bettie, Brother George and I, with my three months old baby, followed. Sister kept Annie for me. We drove to Weatherford in one of those large three-seated hacks or ambulances as they were called. We had a negro boy hostler, and Colonel Gad, a man who was introducing barbed wire for pasture fences, was with us. Father Matthews had given him an order for wire with which to fence his pasture. Colonel Gad was from Des Moines, Iowa, but this wire was being made in Dallas, I think. At any rate they were putting the barbs on it there and the factory must have been there. This was the first wire fence in our part of the country and the posts were iron with a screw on the end for putting them down.

Taking a three months old baby on a jaunt like that seems too foolish for words now, but I can look back upon several such foolish things. I was young and had seen little of life. I have said since that I would never have gone anywhere in my early married life if I had not taken a baby for I could not leave them. There was one advantage, I was not bothered with carrying bottles this time.

We took the train at Weatherford, leaving our hack there. This was the end of the Texas and Pacific Railroad at that time, at least passenger trains were coming only this far. The road was building west rapidly, however, and was a boon to our section of the country.

While on the way to Weatherford, we had dinner with the construction gang in the car used for a diner. We went in and were settled in our places before the men came in and my baby was lying on my lap under the table where she could not be seen. During the meal she set up a lusty cry and those men raised their heads like a bunch of startled deer. They did not know where that strange noise was coming from.

Father had driven down to Weatherford to meet Mother who was getting back from her visit in Alabama. We all met there and had dinner together at the Sikes House, a famous old tavern of early days kept by Widow Sikes, quite a character. Her house was noted for good meals, always served family style. After dinner Mother and Father started west and we boarded the train for Fort Worth where we stayed a day or so having some dresses made by Mrs. Brown. Then we went over to Dallas where the convention for nominating a governor was being held. Our men folks were delegates to this convention as were also Mr. Conrad and Nick Eaton. Governor Roberts was nominated at the convention; he was an old friend and neighbor of my father's in East Texas and naturally we were strong for him, knowing that he was a man of high character and integrity. I think Conrad was for his opponent but I cannot remember who that was now. We stayed in the home of Colonel Gad while in Dallas.

From Dallas we went down into Arkansas and visited with the Matthews' relatives. Sister Bettie and Mother Matthews went on from there to Hot Springs for a time and the rest of us came home. We stopped a few days in Weatherford where we visited in the home of Colonel Buster, an old friend of the family. There were two jolly girls in that family, Sallie, who afterward became Mrs. Couts, and Nannie. They kept things going lively; Sallie played the guitar, sang and was quite a wit. I cannot say that this was a very pleasant trip for me, not very strong and with the care of a young baby which cried a lot as any child would being moved about so much. Aside from that I contracted a bad case of malaria and was very sick after getting home. I know now that I should have far better stayed quietly at home although I did enjoy meeting new people and being in a city. Dallas and Fort Worth both seemed quite like cities to me then though they were little more than good sized villages, but they did have a railroad and were thriving towns. We were away for about a month in all on this trip.

After coming home I developed the malaria and that clung to me for a long time. We would get it checked for a while but it would return periodically. I just could not shake it off altogether and it almost shook the life out of me.

IV

The Tecumseh place was on a public road leading from Albany to Throckmorton, the county seat of Throckmorton County which had been organized in 1879 and adjoins Shackelford County on the north. The county came near being a family affair as to officers. Among the first were Glenn Reynolds, who served as sheriff for one year and resigned, and Flake Barber, the first clerk. At the next election N. L. Bartholomew went in as judge, D. C. Campbell, treasurer, Flake Barber, clerk, and J. A. Matthews, commissioner from our district. Bartholomew and Campbell served out their terms but lived on the ranch.

As there was a lot of passing on this road connecting the two county seats, we had a great deal of company here; some we enjoyed, some we knew only made a convenience of us which was not so pleasant. Judge Fleming, district judge at the time, was a friend of ours whom we enjoyed. He and his retinue of lawyers would spend the night with us on the way from Albany to Throckmorton to hold court. We were only twelve miles from Throckmorton and they could drive there in time to hold court in the morning. Everyone knew the Judge's habit of staying at our home and sometimes the neighbors who had to go to court would drop in for breakfast knowing they would not be late because they would be going with the Judge. One morning, I remember, Uncle William Spears came early and woke us up; he, of course, was privileged and we thought that a rather smart trick. There were two others who came later that morning, one after we had finished breakfast.

We sold this place before very long and moved to the Camp Cooper Ranch which had been vacated by Uncle William who had moved his family to Griffin. Professor Dalrymple had been called to take charge of the school there now. Camp Cooper was not on any road and seemed rather quiet and lonely after having lived where people were passing and dropping in at all times of the day. If any one came, it was solely to visit us. We had plenty of neighbors as nearly every quarter section had a tenant, but there were some who had lived on their land the required length of time, then had sold out to an adjoining family who in that way acquired a large block of land. All these first settlers finally sold to the ranchmen as a farmer could not make a living on a small tract of land; they must have enough to raise a few cattle anyway. This was and still is strictly a cattle country, although there is a lot of farming in some parts. Some counties have much more farming lands than others. A number of the families from this community went to the state of Washington where they did very well in raising fruit, apples principally. The Camp Cooper Ranch had acquired a good bit of this land.

On April 23, 1881, there was another wedding when Ella and Mr. Conrad were married. Mr. Conrad was a widower with one child, Frank B. This was a rather quiet wedding, not so many guests. I hardly see how that could have happened. They went to housekeeping in Fort Griffin.

V

Now comes a time of which it makes my heart ache to write even though more than fifty years have passed. Our little Annie, so lovely, so sweet and promising, loved by all who knew her, was stricken with what the doctors called typhoid dysentery and died May 24, 1881. No one who has not passed through the same sorrow can possibly know the anguish of parting with a child. She was an unusual little girl, so sweet and thoughtful of everyone with whom she came in contact. She was laid under the daisies on the hillside near my father's home where she was born and where she died, the idol of his heart. The sun went under a cloud, the earth turned grey to me. It has been said that the first cut of the surgeon's knife is the most painful, so the first great sorrow is hardest to bear. I believe that is the case for I am sure we are given more fortitude as we grow older, and even then it is hard, so hard that we will wonder why these sorrows come.

Life must go on though hearts are breaking; I had my little May, one year old, to take care of. She was such a blessing for there is nothing like having to get up and do things to alleviate grief. To be compelled to use our hands will divert us to some extent for if we have to use our hands we must of necessity use our minds some, and time will gradually wear the sharp edge of sorrow. This is a kind provision of Providence; if it were not the case we could hardly go on living.

In the fall of this year another wedding occurred in the home of Brother George and Sister Bettie; this time it was Mart Gentry who had been with the family for years and was foreman of the ranch now, and Melissa Merry, a young woman who had been in the home for some time. They were given a nice wedding like that of the brother and cousin who married there. They set up housekeeping for a while in a little house in the neighborhood.

They did not stay there long however; they came back to the home in which they were married and here their first baby was born. Brother George and Sister Bettie had no children and travelled a great deal, so this was a very convenient arrangement for both couples, William and Susie having moved to a home of their own.

About this time a church had been organized in my father's home by that prince of preachers and synodical evangelist of the Presbyterian Church, Dr. H. S. Little, a pioneer of Presbyterianism in West Texas who drove thousands of miles over the country organizing churches and preaching to scattered ranchmen.

In 1879 or '80, wonderful mineral water had been discovered in Palo Pinto County and a town was built there called "Mineral Wells." Many wooden buildings were hastily thrown up comprising hotels and cheap boarding houses for the most part. People flocked there. Father and Mother went down and lived in a tent before any houses were built in the hope of a benefit for Father from the mineral water. He was grasping at straws as sick people do. It did his trouble no good but rather harm as he failed fast after this.

Headstone of Annie Caroline Matthews marked the first grave in the family cemetery in Reynolds Bend.

10   *Moving*

I

In 1880 MART HOOVER, a brother-in-law, decided to move to Kansas where his brother, who was also his partner, lived and where they had interests together. John bought his stock of cattle, horses, and so forth, which was a good sized deal for a young man to put over. After due consideration he decided there was strength in union; this stock having been bought on credit for $50,000, he thought it would be too heavy a burden for one, so a partnership, Reynolds & Matthews was formed. They had been ranching together for a number of years anyway. It was understood that this partnership, after five years, might be dissolved if either party wished.

Now they were beginning to buy land and to fence pastures with wire, and some people fenced land they had neither bought nor leased. This fencing of pastures was a new thing; the people were used to open, free range, letting their cattle roam at will wherever grass and water were best. Feeling ran high for a while because people felt that they were being defrauded of their rights and as a result fences were being cut right and left. The Cattle Raisers Association had been in existence for a few years for the protection and mutual benefit of the cattlemen. The association held a meeting in Austin and influenced the governor, Mr. Ireland, to convoke the Legislature and they passed a law making it a penal offense for anyone to cut fences or to fence land he did not own or have leased. So that ended fence cutting. Incidentally, we never had a foot of wire cut.

Our Tecumseh place which we had sold reverted back to us as the buyer could not pay for it. This was then turned in to Reynolds & Matthews in exchange for the Hoover home on the Clear Fork which the company had bought after the partnership was formed. The first deal made was only for live stock.

The old California Ranch was now abandoned, and as in days of yore, as soon as our cow outfit moved out, a family moved in. In later years it was burned and is now in ruins. I have never seen it since leaving it years ago. We stayed on at Camp Cooper until April, 1882, when we moved to the Hoover place.

II

It was very evident now that Father was not to be with us long; he was failing fast. Dear Father, ever an example of such upright character and Christian manhood to his children and to all who knew him. He was "Uncle Watt" to everyone. He died on the Seventh day of June, 1882, and we buried him on the hill near his beloved little Annie.

Mother came to us now, leaving the home to Bennie and Florence.

On the Twelfth of September, to our great joy, a son was born to us. His father was so delighted that he mounted his horse the next morning and galloped around the neighborhood shouting the news of the arrival of Joe B. Matthews, II. Grandchildren were coming in hordes now; within one year there were five grandsons born into the Matthews family. We seemed to be obeying the Lord's command to Noah after the flood: "Be fruitful, and multiply, and replenish the earth." We were doing our part in populating this country.

THE HOOVER HOUSE,
built in 1875 by Martin V. Hoover, a brother-in-law
of John Alexander Matthews, was one of the family
residences built on the Clear Fork. It became the
property of John and Sallie Matthews in 1880.

When Bennie and Florence married, they took a trip to Arkansas, and when they came home they brought another Matthews girl with them, Florence's sister, Rosa. In due time as a consequence of this visit, there was another tie made between the two families. On March 20, 1883, Phin Reynolds and Rosa Matthews were united in marriage.

Again there was a gathering of the clan to celebrate the wedding of this, the youngest and last brother. This was an unusual union of two families: two pairs of sisters, first cousins to each other, married to my four brothers, and I married to the only brother of one pair of sisters. We were surely being interwoven.

III

This summer Reynolds & Matthews were pasturing some cattle in Kansas near Hunnewell, and when the time came for shipping them to market John planned to go up and take me and the children, May and Joe.

As I was still having chills at intervals, we decided we would first try the mineral waters recently discovered in Palo Pinto County and becoming very popular, the now famous Mineral Wells. There were some who thought the water a remedy for all the ills of life. We spent ten days there and as I have never had a touch of malaria since that time, I naturally think it the sovereign remedy for malaria at least.

We were joined in Fort Worth by Brother George and Sister Bettie; they had with them Lula Matthews, an orphaned niece of Father Matthews', age nine, whom they had taken to raise. An older sister, Minnie, was in the home of William and Susie, while we had Dave, a brother.

From Fort Worth we went to Kansas City, Missouri, that being convenient to Hunnewell, from where the cattle were shipped

into the Kansas City market. We spent several weeks very pleas-
antly at the old St. James Hotel where Brother had had the
arrowhead removed the year before.

IV

After we returned home, Brother George became restless and
tired of the isolation of ranch life, so he and Sister Bettie went
into Albany and spent the winter at the Barnes House. This was
a very comfortable hotel for that time, and there were a number
of pleasant people there.

Albany, the county seat of Shackelford County, was then the
terminus of the Texas Central Railroad. F. E. Conrad had moved
his store from Fort Griffin to this place and there were other
stores; Meyers of Fort Griffin had moved his store to the railroad,
B. W. Rose was in the mercantile business here, and N. H. Burns
in the hardware business, but there was no bank in the town.
In 1883 a few of the progressive citizens of the country decided
to organize one. G. T. Reynolds, W. D. Reynolds, R. E. McAnulty,
E. P. Davis, who lived in Throckmorton County, N. L. Bartholomew, F. E. Conrad and J. R. Fleming, former district judge now
practicing law in Albany, were the founders. Fleming was made
president and Bartholomew cashier. It was organized as a private
bank and called The Albany Bank, and continued under that
name until July 24, 1884, when it became The First National
Bank of Albany, Texas. Being cashier of course brought Brother
Barney to town. This work suited him much better than farming
and stock raising. He was well equipped by education for his
position as cashier of a bank and looked the part, being dignified
and at all times well groomed. Fleming served only a short time
as president, being succeeded in the latter part of 1884 by Brother
George, who held the office until 1905 when the presidency was
turned over to Bartholomew, "Uncle Barney" as he was affec-

tionately called. When he resigned because of age, our son, Joe B. Matthews, II, was made president.

Brother Barney had traded his place on the Clear Fork to Mart Dixon for his farm near town; it was just across the creek on the south. Here they had every advantage of town and country life, the house being only a short distance from the courthouse square, with the farm behind it and the little creek with its timber screening it from the public in front. The creek would sometimes get up and cut him off from the bank for a few hours, but he soon remedied that by building a foot bridge. The house was on rather low ground, very near the creek. He had it raised several feet and filled the yard in with soil so the house was out of danger from high water. The children and young people of the family had many picnics on "Uncle Barney's creek" as they called it. This home was always open to the young people; I believe they were entertained more often here than in any other home in town. The nephews and nieces all called Sister "Aunt Sister." My brother, Glenn, started his boy, Elmer, who was her first nephew, to saying, "Aunt Sister" and all the others followed. There were so many of the real nieces and nephews getting to be about that soon the whole town, young and old, were saying "Uncle Barney" and "Aunt Sister."

Sister and Brother Barney now had a little adopted daughter growing up with the other nieces and nephews, May Vernon Bartholomew.

When the family once started the move to town there was a real exodus, the ranches were deserted, Bennie being the only one of the family to stay on the ranch.

John Brown, a Presbyterian minister who had married our sister, Mary, and had been engaged in the sheep business for a while, was called to the pastorate of the Presbyterian Church at Albany. With the relatives who were already in Albany,

namely, Uncle William Spears with two married children, making three families, and my father's niece, Mrs. Bob Coffee, and
her family which included her father, my Uncle Ben, who was
living with them, there was indeed an army of relatives. It was
said of us that those who were not kin to us were kin to our kin-
folk, and sometimes that fact was used against us in elections.

We came to Albany the Seventh of July and on the Fifteenth
of October our dear little Susette was born, our fourth child.
She was christened Susan Elizabeth for her three aunts, my sister,
Susan, Sister Bettie and Susie Reynolds. We wanted to call her
for all so ran it into Susette.

About this time the Tonkawas were moved into the Indian
Territory and now old Fort Griffin was completely deserted, the
soldiers all having been moved away a year or two earlier, I
cannot remember the exact dates. Lieutenant Chandler was
Indian Agent at the time. After the removal of the soldiers
from Fort Griffin the country seemed rather deserted; we missed
the life and stir of a military post but there was no reason now
for their staying as Indians troubled us no more. The removal of
the fort may have been one cause of our all going to Albany.

v

The Cotton Exposition was on in New Orleans the spring of
1885 and a party of us went down for it. Mother and Father
Matthews, the G. T. and W. D. Reynolds, the R. E. McAnultys,
Ben Reynolds, and John and I made up the party. Susie, Mrs.
McAnulty and I each had a baby about the same age and each
had a nurse. Counting the babies and the nurses there were
seventeen in the party. We left Albany the Fifteenth of February
and reached New Orleans in time for the Mardi Gras crush.

With both the Exposition and the Mardi Gras on, the city
was overflowing and it was difficult to find lodgings for so many

people in one house, since we had no reservations. Nevertheless we finally found a place on Carondelet Street where we had rooms and breakfast in one of the big, old-fashioned homes. The accommodations were none too good but people raised on the frontier were not bothered. The women and babies had two rooms, as I remember. They were large rooms with open fires and we were comfortable enough.

The exposition grounds were eight miles from the city on the river and every morning we would take a boat for the grounds. This was the first time I had ever seen this great river, up which my mother had sailed on her first trip to Texas almost forty years before. I thoroughly enjoyed these boat rides up and down it. When we would get out to the grounds, we would park our nurses and babies in some convenient location in one of the buildings where the nurses could see something of the show and the babies would be comfortable. We would wander around, seeing the wonders of the exposition, coming back at regular intervals to nurse the babies. We were most foolish in taking those young babies, only a few months old, into such a place but this was not the last time we took them with us.

William, who had never had measles, picked up the germ somewhere, we never knew how nor when the contact was made, and of course this could have happened at any other time in his travels about the country. When we came home he made the rounds to the different ranches and line camps. He began feeling sick, had a little fever and came in home, stopping at Griffin for dinner on his way in. The next morning they called in the doctor and after examining him, he pronounced it measles. It was coming out well then. In his visits to the different places he had scattered the disease well, not dreaming of any contagion. From that the whole country had measles. His own children were very sick.

VI

The Chautauqua Literary and Scientific Circle was becoming known in the country and getting to be very popular in the East. Professor Dalrymple, Miss Bettie Parker, Mrs. N. H. Burns and a few others had organized a circle in Albany, and I was very glad indeed to avail myself of the educational advantage of this study course which was well chosen and excellent in those early years. This was a small circle but a live one. We met every Friday afternoon at four o'clock at the schoolhouse. I shall never cease to be thankful for that first little study circle, one among the first in the State, having been organized in 1883. Not having been to school since I was fourteen years of age, I felt the need of some regular course of study. Bishop Vincent did a lot for the country when he founded the C. L. S. C.; I for one render to him sincere thanks and I am sure he has his reward. I feel that I obtained a lot out of this course of study and the contacts and helpful association.

The family as a whole took an interest in all the work of the Church; the children went regularly to Sunday school and to church as soon as they were old enough. Mr. Brown organized a Ladies' Missionary Society in 1886, one of the first in the State, and it has gone on all these years without a break. There are six of those first members still living but I am the only one who lives in Albany and who is still a member. While we were away for a time we never severed our connection with the Mother Church.

For a small town, Albany has been a rather up-to-date town in every way and there has always been a fine class of people here. At one time they had a dramatic club, "The Shakespeare Dramatic Club," which put on some very creditable perform-ances. Mrs. Crump, a music teacher, was the leading spirit in this. She gathered the musical and histrionic talent of the town into this club.

After moving to Albany we bought a piano and I took up the study of music again with Mrs. Searcy, a very good teacher, although she was never able to make a musician out of me; still I struggled with it and felt repaid even though I never made a pianist. I think any effort to improve oneself along any line helps and is that much. I also dabbled with paints, never making an artist but getting a lot of pleasure out of trying.

Another wedding in the family was brewing between my sister's only child, Gus Newcomb, and Minnie Matthews who made her home with William and Susie. On April 29, 1886, there was a quiet wedding in that home when Gus and Minnie took the marriage vows; Mr. Brown performed the ceremony with only the family and a few friends present.

VII

In the year of 1885, the sheep men of this country went broke almost to a man. This, of course, was laid at the feet of Democratic administration, Cleveland having been elected President in 1884. The tariff on wool had been removed and there was no sale for it here except at starvation price. Since wool was worth nothing, some of the sheep owners decided to ship their sheep to the Chicago market and see if they were worth anything as food. E. Frankel shipped several carloads and they netted him one dollar and seventy-five cents per dozen. This was a little better than some others did. Arendt and Shelton made a shipment and the commission firm to which they shipped drew back on them for money, the sheep not quite having paid all charges. That was the status of the sheep business at that time.

Mr. Jess Ellison sold his ranch near Albany to Mr. Edward Stevens, late of England, and moved to Arizona, taking a herd of cattle out there to try the business in a new territory. Glenn, who had been in the sheep business for several years and had

gone broke like all the sheep men, decided to go out to Arizona
with Mr. Ellison. The family, who stand by each other through
thick and thin, fair weather and foul, now chipped in and helped
him to get a nice little bunch of young cows. These he threw in
with Mr. Ellison's cattle and he was put in charge of the herd
to take them to Arizona. Leaving them there in Mr. Ellison's
care, he came back and took another herd out for Reynolds
Brothers the following year. These were taken to the Holbrook
country where he was joined by his family. Gus Newcomb, who
had been married only a short time, went out with this drive,
expecting to locate in Arizona and have his wife come out later.
He changed his mind for some reason and came back home;
perhaps the country was not so alluring after seeing it. Things
have a way of seeming "better further on."

The Ellison herd was taken up into the Mogollon mountain
range on the edge of Tonto Basin, a most beautiful slope under
the fringe of the Mogollons and near the "Pleasant Valley"
country. Mr. Ellison located his family here in the upper edge
of the Basin near the town of Payson which was little more than
a post office. In the year of 1887, a most bloody feudal war raged
between the two families of Tewksbury and Graham and was
called "The Pleasant Valley War," ably described by Zane Grey
in his book, *To the Last Man.* This was a terrible state of affairs,
worse, if possible, than Indian times in West Texas. No one was
safe and feeling ran high. Our people kept on the outside as
much as possible and tried to steer clear of trouble, but even so,
one was almost forced to side with one faction or the other. The
Government took no hand in trying to settle this trouble, as I
remember; it just let them alone until they killed each other out
"to the last man."

Having left the Reynolds cattle in charge of someone there,
my brother had moved his family up from Holbrook to a place

near the Ellisons before this war started. It was an isolated section and there were desperate men roving about; when Glenn rode off in the morning, Gustie had little assurance of seeing him ride back at evening time. In 1887 my brother, Phin, went out to Arizona to close out the Reynolds cattle, and the Pleasant Valley country was in such a state of war that he did not dare to venture into the mountains to see his brother. This trouble was confined to the one section, but the whole state was affected of course.

VIII

Eighteen-eighty-five was the end of the five years' term agreed upon when the partnership was formed between Reynolds and Matthews. Although there had been no business troubles, they having been agreeable with each other, John decided to withdraw, feeling that he might become too dependent upon the older men of the firm. He wanted to try his own right arm, so land and cattle were divided. The firm in this five years had acquired and fenced quite a body of land. Some of this land naturally was more valuable than other, some of it being strictly for grazing and not good for farming. We were willing to take fewer acres and some of the better land. The south land came to us, but "springs of water" were lacking.

This pasture was added to later by purchasing the pasture controlled by a company of sheep men, Culver, Scheuber, Frankel and Chapin. The latter pasture we named "The Culver" for Dr. Culver, one of the owners and our first family physician.

This land was a fine addition to our other pasture and there was a choice piece of land adjoining it known as Lambshead Valley, being located on the Clear Fork just above the point where Lambshead Creek runs into it. The valley, consisting of several sections, had been bought or acquired from the State in an early day by Colonel Stem, an Army officer and Indian agent stationed at old Fort Belknap. The patents were issued in 1853 and 1854. He built a house and put in a farm here, which was an easy matter as he only had to plow a furrow and plant the seed; there was nothing on it but mesquite grass, not a tree or stump. The land was exceedingly rich. In Parker's *Notes Taken* I read that Colonel Stem employed eight men to put in a crop and sold the crop on the ground for forty-three hundred dollars.

This fertile valley probably did not cost Colonel Stem over ten cents an acre, perhaps as much as twenty-five. Colonel Stem was killed in the fall of 1854 by a roving band of Kickapoo Indians. The manner in which these Indians were punished, as told by W. B. Parker in his notes on an expedition made through the country in the summer and fall of 1854, is so interesting that I want to copy them in full.

The punishment of these murderers is an instance of the manner in which justice is done among this barbarous people. From information given by a boy who was with the Indians at the time the murders were committed, the commanding officer at Fort Arbuckle sent for the Kickapoo chiefs and told them the murderers must be given up, at the same time a large reward was offered for their apprehension.

The chiefs told him that they had been in council all night upon the matter; that they knew the murders had been committed by two of their band, who were absent on assembling the men of the tribe, and that they had sent their people out by threes in search, so that any person meeting one Kickapoo alone, or two in company, might immediately arrest him or them. In a short time one of the murderers was arrested by his own people, firmly bound and placed on horseback to be taken into the fort. A short distance from that place, he managed to free himself from his bonds, and throwing himself from the horse attempted to escape, but was immediately shot down and his dead body carried in and delivered to the officer in command. The other made his escape, but after eluding pursuit for a time made his way to a village where his brother lived. Entering this, he commenced exclaiming in a loud voice, "I am the murderer of Colonel Stem, will no one take me and deliver me up for punishment?" In this way he reached his brother's lodge, entering which, he said, "My brother, I committed this murder. I am tired of life. I am hunted down like a wild beast, and I want to die. I tried to join the Comanches but would have starved to death before I could have found them." Food was set before him, of which he partook. His brother and he then walked out of the village, when the former said to him, "My brother, you have disgraced our tribe, and it is my duty to kill you. I have all along told you that your course of life would lead you to this, and however painful it may be to me, yet justice demands the sacrifice. I must kill you." Stepping behind him he then felled him to the earth with his tomahawk, and with repeated blows dispatched him. A council was then held, at which the brother made a speech, stating what he had done, and why, ending by calling a volunteer to behead the body and take the head into the fort, as the distance was too great and the weather too hot to take the whole corpse. No one volunteering, he then said, "I must do it myself," which he did, and carried the head to Fort Arbuckle, where it was buried. Such is Indian justice.

It is rather high flown language, I would say, for one of a wild uncultured race, but it is copied verbatim from Parker's *Notes Taken*, a little book published in 1855.

Colonel Stem was buried at old Fort Belknap and his wife with her four little girls went back to Ohio to her father who helped her raise her family. She never returned to this country.

When we came into possession of the Culver pasture, John immediately began negotiations with Mrs. Stem to lease this valley of hers and terms were agreed upon, and the land put under fence. All these years there would be an occasional exchange of letters, their business dealings being the most pleasant. Judging from her letters, Mrs. Stem was a cultured, refined woman. After Mrs. Stem's death, twenty-five years after this lease was made, we bought the land from her heirs. Mr. Cook, a son-in-law who lived in Cleveland, came down to look the property over and make the deal. After leasing the land all these years, we bought it for twelve dollars per acre. John had always had great respect for Mrs. Stem and felt an interest in her family, and on one of our visits to Cleveland we hunted up Mrs. Cook and called on her. Mr. Cook had died the year before.

In 1886 there was a severe drouth and farmers had a complete failure of crops. Cattlemen were short of grass and some lacked water which was even worse. Cattle can live on leaves and other herbage, but they must have water. There was much shifting about among the cattlemen. Money was a scarce article just now. John decided he would run up to Chetopa, Kansas, and see if he could make a loan with Mart and Will Hoover. He came in one afternoon at four o'clock and asked if I would like to go to Kansas the next day. Of course I was up and ready for a trip. There was a revival meeting on and I was dressed to go to the four o'clock service; so we went on to church, then drove across the creek for Mother who was at my sister's, to stay with the children. We had a good maid to leave with them, too.

The train left at five o'clock in the morning and we were off on it. This trip was somewhat of a lark to me, if times were hard, and we called it our "bridal tour" afterward as we were taken for a bride and groom a time or two. We had a nice little visit with Mart and Mattie, but drew no loan there. In the meantime, Brother George had gone to Kansas City on the same business, intending to go from there to Monroe City, Missouri, where most of the members of the Monroe Cattle Company were living. This company, of which he was president and general manager, had been organized in Texas some years before and was operated here, having large holdings of lands and cattle in this part of the country.

After failing to make a loan in Chetopa, John decided to meet Brother in Monroe City and talk things over with him, so wired Jim Scott to let him know if G. T. Reynolds were there, and if so, to keep him until we could come. He answered in the affirmative. While we had never been to Monroe City, we knew most of the members of the Cattle Company as they came down every year for the stockholders' meetings, always bringing some of the wives, and we usually entertained some of them in our home. So we went right on up after receiving the message. Mr. and Mrs. Jim Scott, Brother George and Sister Bettie met us at the station, not knowing what the matter in hand was. In their talk later, John asked him if he knew of anyone in Kansas City who would lend money. He replied that he did not, that he had utterly failed to get any, and said, "You had just as well go back home." Well, we stayed for a few days and had a delightful visit with the Scotts and Proctors, who were very hospitable and treated us royally. They made up a circus party one day and took us to Hannibal to see Barnum and Bailey's show. They made our stay as pleasant as possible in every way. Nothing was said to them of the business, of course. After our little visit we all left, Brother and Sister going on some of their yearly tours, I do not know just where now, while we started for home. John was feeling a bit low and discouraged. I was not very much cast down for I had the utmost confidence in his ability to work things out some way or somehow, being naturally of a lighthearted and hopeful temperament anyway.

On the train we met a friend, Colonel Casey, a cattleman who liver near Clinton, Missouri, and who had been in Texas some. He was sitting in our section chatting when a rather young man came along. After Colonel Casey had introduced him to us and he had passed on, John asked what business he was in. Casey replied that his business was loaning money on land; he was Herman P. Faris, junior member of the firm of Brinkerhoff-Faris Trust and Savings Company of Clinton, Missouri. This meeting seemed providential at the time. John told Colonel Casey that that was the business that had brought him to Missouri, and he immediately began negotiations with Faris for a loan. Faris promised to come down and look at the land and he did so very soon, bringing Mr. Brinkerhoff with him. Twenty-five thousand dollars was borrowed from this company at straight ten per cent interest, twelve per cent commission, and oh, what a vulture that ten per cent was, eating our very vitals. This company took a blanket mortgage on our whole ranch. John always thought Coloney Casey had said a good word for him. The business associations with Mr. Faris have always been the most friendly and pleasant, and the friendship formed through this business has continued down the years.

IX

This year of dearth, Rev. John Brown conceived the idea of calling on the Red Cross which had not long been established in the United States. He made a trip to Washington to see what could be done, and was instrumental in having Miss Clara Barton come down. I believe she came home with him, anyway, she came, bringing her general field agent, Dr. Julian Hubbell. They established headquarters in Brother George's home and began a personal and systematic investigation of the situation in the drouth stricken area.

This paragraph from a letter written to her sister at that time shows her methods and personal feelings.

Albany, Texas
Feb. 3rd, '87

Dear Fannie:

I have not time to tell you how it is, but you may be sure it is bad enough. The Dr. and I left Washington the last of the month, have been here some days travelling, met the people, learned their necessities in their own homes and have done what we could in so short a time to make ourselves acquainted with the needs that lie upon them. The sum of one hundred thousand dollars has just been appropriated by the Legislature of this State for food which will do something toward providing for their present wants. Much more will be needed for clothing and household comforts before another crop could possibly be raised even if the rains make a good season which is questionable.

After she had been driven over the country, going into the homes of the farmers and seeing the need there, a mass meeting was called at the courthouse and there Clara Barton told us things. She was most kind and sympathetic and she realized that there was want and distress, but having recently been in the flooded districts of the Mississippi where the devastation was exceedingly great, she felt that the situation here was not so calamitous in comparison. She gave us to understand that the Red Cross was not supposed to aid except in great disasters such as floods, earthquakes and other dire calamities, that Texas was too big and too resourceful to be calling for help outside the State. She also said that much of the money contributed to the Red Cross was the hard earned pennies of very poor people in the East, and intimated that we did not know what hard work was as the New Englander knew it, and that we were not thrifty and provident as they were. This she had learned, no doubt, from their visits in the homes. I think most of us agreed with her there. My recollection now is that Texas managed the drouth situation without help from any source outside the State.

Albany was honored in having such a noble and distinguished guest as "The Angel of the Battlefield." Miss Barton was an intelligent woman, a wise woman, a strong forceful speaker, pleasant and unassuming in manner as all really great people are. As she was in my brother's home I had the privilege of knowing her personally, and a very great privilege it was. Life must necessarily be enriched by even a light contact with a character like Clara Barton, and when she kissed me goodbye it was like a benediction.

x

On Christmas day, 1886, we celebrated our tenth wedding anniversary. I wrote to Mrs. C. D. Brown, who attended to anything for us from making dresses and mounting needle point slippers to buying wedding cards, asking her to send me cards for invitations; these were of a color and texture resembling tin. We did not send out many cards, but had all the family and a few special friends in for dinner. Later on in the afternoon (we had dinner in the middle of the day) I put on my wedding dress to the surprise of some of the family who, thinking I had grown entirely too matronly, had no idea I could get into it as I was such a slim sapling when I married; but I fooled them and sported around in it which seemed to please the guests. John put on his wedding suit and we stood up together for awhile but did not have a ceremony repeated, though we could have had as there were two preachers there, Rev. John Wallace, Methodist, who happened to be a friend of some of the family, and Mr. Brown. I look back on this as one of the very nicest parties we ever had in our home.

In the fall of the next year, on the 28th of August, another little girl came to our home, Ethel, born on the Sabbath day. The little rhyme says,

> *"The child that is born on the Sabbath day*
> *Is bonnie and blythe and good and gay."*

She was all that, a bonnie little girl. We could not realize then how we were being blessed in these fair daughters, three now. Their father would often jokingly say, "the devil owes me a debt and will pay it off in sons-in-law." This did not prove true, however, as we have a splendid lot of sons-in-law, not a black sheep in the whole flock.

II   *Back to the Ranch*

I

TIMES WERE GETTING HARD with us now; the Culver pasture and other lands had been bought with money borrowed for that purpose. While we were getting land we were also getting a burden of debt, so John thought it expedient that we should go back to the ranch in order to cut down expenses. His being on the ranch would do away with the salary of a foreman; furthermore it would lessen household expenses as we could live much more cheaply there. So, although our older children were drawing near school age, we moved back. We left Albany October 16, 1887, on a cold misty day, but we had a good comfortable carriage with curtains buttoned down and consequently did not suffer with cold on the thirty mile drive. We had a good woman to help with the housework and care of the children, and two faithful retainers at the ranch, J. D. Overton and Francis Gober who was a member of our household for many years.

This fall there was a fine crop of pecans and there was a very good market for them; the merchants bought them and shipped them out in car loads. Up to this time a crop of pecans had been almost worthless as there had been no market for them. This crop, coming after the drouth, was worth a lot to the country;

those who had no pecan trees could gather on the shares from those who did. From now on a crop of pecans was a source of revenue in the country.

The morning of the Seventeenth dawned bright and sunny, with the ground white from the frozen mist of the day before, but the sun soon melted it. We gathered the whole family and had an outing on the river, harvesting pecans. This we did for several days, since the weather made it pleasant to be out. All enjoyed these days on the river, even baby Ethel who lay on her bed under a tree, looking with interest at the quivering leaves which had not yet fallen. She was watched over by her dear Grandmother Reynolds, while we all busied ourselves picking up the fine nuts. We stayed at the ranch through the winter even though we did not move everything out until spring.

The next year the citizens of this community, Bennie, Mart Dixon, Mart Gentry and John, built a schoolhouse in the Bend near Father's old home, then occupied by my brother, Bennie. There were only a few children of school age, but we must begin with the few. The first school-mistress was Miss Esther Hutton from Archer County; her family were from Wisconsin and had not long been in the country. She was an excellent teacher and a resourceful young woman. She stayed in our home and carried our children back and forth to school. The Gentrys, who lived just across the river from us, would bring Mary over and she would go to school with our children. We had a little one-horse buck-board which had an extension in the back, large enough to put three or four children in. Miss Hutton would load up, with gentle

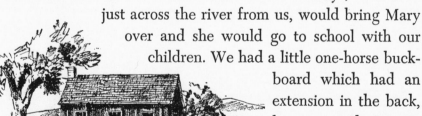

Schoolhouse in Reynolds Bend

"Frio" in the shafts, and away they would go. We kept two Waddell boys who lived too far away to attend this school. The schoolhouse was not too far from our home for them to walk which they often did when the weather was fine, but since the children were young, they usually rode.

When the schoolhouse was built, we organized a small Sunday school, which all attended regularly, old and young. A Methodist minister from Throckmorton would come down and give us a sermon now and then.

This year, 1888, the Synod of the Presbyterian Church, U.S.A., in Texas, met in Albany in October and the Women's Synodical and Presbyterial met at the same time. We went over for that important event. There certainly was a fine body of men there for that meeting, Dr. Wright of Austin, Dr. Smith of Crockett, Dr. McClelland, President of Daniel Baker College, Brownwood, Dr. Riggs, "the Beloved," of Dallas, our own Dr. Little, Dr. Scudder, missionary to India, and many others whose names I cannot recall now. This was an outstanding meeting of the state and I think the preachers were agreeably surprised by the small frontier town. These Presbyterians were the ones who gave Albany the name of "The Preachers' Paradise."

The high officials of the Women's Auxiliaries were here also and their business meetings were held in the Cumberland Church. At one of these sessions my mother was asked to tell them something about early days in the West, which she did. She told about the "Hardshell" Preacher Clarke coming out once every month on foot to preach, of the Methodist circuit riders who came later, and other incidents. Then, in her quiet gentle manner, she said, "There were no Presbyterians who came in those early days; I do not know if they were afraid of Indians or did not think there were enough of us to be worth coming after." One of the visiting men, Dr. Rankin of the American Bible

Society, had come in to hear what the women had to say, and he did not appreciate the last remark very much, as he afterward asked Brother Barney if his mother-in-law was not a little eccentric. I think Dr. Little would have enjoyed the little speech immensely.

After having the pleasure of attending this meeting of Synod, we went back to the ranch, taking up the usual routine of life in the country. We had moved a part of our household goods out in the spring, the main thing being the piano. Mr. Hollowell, father of our townsman, Luther Hollowell, had taken the responsibility of moving it for us and did it with a great deal of care. It was a thirty mile haul over a rough, rocky road, and he delivered it in good shape. The transporting of such heavy pieces of furniture then was somewhat of a problem, owing to bad roads, steep hills and creek banks for there were no bridges. We sold our home in town, partly furnished, to F. E. Conrad, our brother-in-law.

We made some improvements on the house* in the country, adding a large kitchen and storeroom, and turning the little old kitchen and dining room into one fair size room.

At this time Christmas was drawing near so we had to get ready for the children's Christmas tree. This necessitated a trip to town, so Mrs. Gentry, my good neighbor, and I drove in together. The trip took two days altogether. We saw about Santa Claus, made our purchases and started for home on the second day. When we got within about twelve miles of the ranch, in going up a hill one tug broke. If you children do not know what a tug is, it is a strong thick piece of leather that fastens to the hames that are around the horse's collar, and has a hole in the end that hooks to the singletree, and probably you will not know what that is. Well, this hole that held the singletree broke, and we were twelve miles from home. We got out to take a look at

* The Hoover Place.

the broken harness, then set to work to remedy it. Mrs. Gentry had a tiny little knife, very dull, but we cut and worked on that hard piece of leather until we had made a new hole in it large enough to slip onto the end of the singletree. We reached home before dark caught us, although a bit late.

This Christmas I made a lot of the children's things, including cloth scrap-books of pink and blue glazed cambric with pinked edges in which the little ones enjoyed pasting pictures, canton flannel animals of various kinds, goats, elephants, mice, horses and others. Six year old Joe was very pleased with a brown canton flannel pony all saddled and bridled, with shoe buttons for eyes and old-fashioned straight clothespins, put in with knob end down, for legs. He loved horses from the time he could walk. The children were happy with their simple presents.

II

The next spring John took cattle up into the Cherokee Strip of the Indian Territory to pasture and get ready for market later. He sent one of his men, Carter, with a train and he himself went with another, having John Bennett with him. They went through Oklahoma the night before that famous signal gun was fired that opened three million acres of land to actual settlers. There were camp fires in a half mile wide strip all along the railroad line, and people tumbling over each other off the passenger trains to be ready for a quick getaway when the signal should be given. It must have been an exciting time.

The cattle were unloaded at a station called Chilocco near the line of Kansas not far from Arkansas City. Here the cattle were taken to pasture where he left them with Jack Carter to look after them as that was the agreement with the man who took them to pasture, that he leave one of his own men whose wages would be paid by the owner of the pasture. This was a very satisfactory arrangement. Our old Texas friend, Nick Eaton, now married and living in Kansas City, was pasturing cattle with the same man.

This summer we had another wedding, that of Miss Alice Lyons from Tennessee, who had been making her home with Mother Matthews for some time, and one of the men on our ranch, J. D. Overton. The wedding was at Father Matthews', and the families all came out for it, including the children, as everyone was fond of Miss Alice, and we were pleased with the match. The next day they came on up to our ranch which was his home, and we had a neighborhood picnic and fish fry in their honor.

Later on this summer when the time came to ship the cattle to market we went to Arkansas City, Kansas, taking May and Joe, who were now nine and seven, respectively. We left the two younger children at the ranch in charge of Mr. and Mrs. Overton who had with them Mrs. Crowson and Mrs. Roxie Johnson, two faithful helpers who lived with us. The G. T. Reynolds, Mother Matthews and Mrs. Willie LeMonde were with us. We made a short stay at Arkansas City, then went to Gueda Springs, a small watering place nearby. There was a very good hotel there and we spent a few days before going on to Kansas City, Missouri. Here our companions left us and went to Fall River, Massachusetts, to visit the Browns who were living there, Mr. Brown being pastor of a church there.

Mr. and Mrs. Eaton came over to the station to see the party off and to take us home with them. They had a very nice home out on Vine and Linwood, near Troost Avenue Park, and near them lived Tom Bugbee, another Texas ranchman. We spent a very pleasant week with the Eatons. They had a large yard and garden, and the children enjoyed them and the park near at hand. Mrs. Eaton was a Miss Mamie Gill, of one of the old families of Kansas City.

We went back to Arkansas City after one lot of cattle had been sent in to market. They brought such a scandalously low price that John sold the others in the pasture, range delivery, and we came home, having had a pleasant summer trip if not a profitable one.

III

When Gila County, Arizona, was organized my brother, Glenn, was elected sheriff. On November 2, 1889, he was most foully murdered. My brave splendid brother, who had grown to manhood amid the dangers of frontier life in Texas, now was cut down in the prime of his young manhood, being only thirty-five years old. He, with only one guard, his deputy, Holmes, was taking eight convicted Indians and one Mexican to the penitentiary at Yuma; among them was "the Apache Kid," fiend incarnate. My brother had asked for another guard, but there was none forthcoming, so he left Globe with all these prisoners, and only the one other guard. Details of the tragedy are contained in the following newspaper account.

VICTIMS OF APACHES

DETAILS OF THE TRAGIC AFFRAY
In Which Glenn Reynolds Met An Untimely Death
From *The Arizona Silver Belt*

(Knowing that very few of the many friends of Mr. Glenn Reynolds have had an opportunity to read a full account of his sad death, we publish the following, which is reliable.)

This community was thrown into a state of great excitement and consternation last Saturday, about noon, by the arrival of S. C. Taylor with the dreadful report that Sheriff Glenn Reynolds of Gila County, and W. A. Holmes, who left Globe on the previous morning with a Mexican and eight Indian convicts, whom they were conveying to Yuma for incarceration in the Territorial prison, had been overpowered and murdered, and Eugene Middleton badly wounded, by the Apache prisoners.

The startling news was accepted as authentic, notwithstanding that it seemed incredible that such a calamity could have befallen men of known bravery and experience as were Reynolds and Holmes. A posse composed of Deputy Sheriff Ryan, Aran, Roberts, Fowler, Paredes and Blevins, started almost immediately for the scene of tragedy, about four miles west of Riverside. Several versions of the killing, all different somewhat in material points, were received, and it is doubtful if the exact and complete details of the dreadful affair will be known until the perpetrators of the crime are apprehended and have told their story. The account given by the Mexican prisoner, Jesús Avott, in connection with Eugene Middleton's story is sufficiently clear and full, however, to leave no doubt that Reynolds and Holmes were surprised by six of their Indian prisoners.

The facts are about as follows: The party left Globe on the morning of Nov. 1st. The Indian prisoners, eight in number, were placed in one large coach drawn by four horses. Eugene Middleton, driver, W. A. Holmes, deputy sheriff, and Jesús Avott, the Mexican prisoner, were on horseback. All went well until Riverside was passed, where the party staid overnight and resumed their journey on the morning of the 2nd, before daylight.

Upon reaching the foot of a long grade, heavy with sand, about four miles beyond Riverside, in order to lighten the coach, six Indians were taken out, and all the accounts received agree that they were shackled three abreast, the legs of each of the two in the middle were fastened to the inside leg of a prisoner on either side of him, and their hands were similarly secured, the outside prisoners each having an arm and leg free.

This statement, however, is positively denied by Deputy Sheriff Ryan who says that Sheriff Reynolds had only three pair of shackles when the party left Globe, and when they reached the long wash where the revolt occurred two pair of shackles were put upon the legs of the two prisoners in the coach and the third pair were fastened upon one leg of the Mexican, thus leaving the six prisoners on foot entirely without shackles, and they being simply handcuffed in pairs.

The party began the ascent of the wash in the following order: First the coach, driven by Middleton, with Kid and another Indian on the inside, shackled but not together; a short distance behind walked the Mexican, Jesús Avott; then Reynolds, and behind him the six prisoners, and Holmes and those in front of him, when they started, but it is presumed that the officers allowed what they considered a safe distance to intervene between themselves and their treacherous prisoners; but as they proceeded, the Indians must have stealthily diminished the space separating them, until within a few feet of the officers, when those behind Reynolds grappled with him, and at the same time other prisoners turned suddenly upon Holmes and caught him before he had time to bring his Winchester into play.

The above were the positions of the officers and their prisoners, when the Mexican, hearing the scuffle, turned, and seeing that the Indians had surprised the officers, and being unarmed himself, he ran forward and shouted to Middleton "for God's sake let me in." Avott claims that he was shot at three times. Kid and his companions, with a yell, attempted to get out of the coach which was then about one hundred yards in front of Reynolds in the murderous grasp of the three Indians, and Holmes, struggling with the other Indians, must have been fifty feet behind Reynolds as their bodies were found about that distance apart. Middleton turned and covered Kid with his pistol and made him resume his seat, but the other Indians escaped from the coach, ran back to the scene of affray, secured— it is believed—Reynolds' shot gun and ran up again on one side of the road near the coach and as Middleton leaned out and looked back to see what the trouble was, he received a shot in the right cheek, the bullet passing through the face and neck without striking a bone, and came out at the back of the neck, narrowly missing the vertebrae. It was a close call and as it was, Middleton was stunned and fell to the ground, face down, and while conscious, with rare presence of mind lay motionless and limp while the Indian devils stripped off his coat and rifled his pockets. They even examined his wounds and evidently concluding that it was fatal, left him without inflicting additional injury. The Mexican, horses and coach, in the meantime, had passed over the summit and out of sight. The Indian Kid had jumped from the coach and joined his confederates.

The manner of shooting of Middleton is disputed. Middleton himself stated that the Indian who escaped from the coach when the trouble began ran back, secured Reynolds' gun and returned within a short distance (one report says 25 feet) of the coach and shot him from a bush on the side of the road. It seems improbable, however, that Middleton would have been struck by only one shot from a gun loaded with buckshot, fired at so short a range. Dr. J. W. Largent, who went to Riverside to attend Middleton, examined his wounds and gives it as his opinion that it was inflicted by a small caliber rifle ball. To further support this belief is the fact that the Indian who first jumped from the coach was shackled and it would have required some minutes for him to have gone back where the struggle was and returned with a gun and fired at Middleton. The theory that one of the

Indians who murdered Holmes shot Middleton with Holmes' rifle (a 40-80)
is more plausible.

Reynolds, evidently, made a desperate attempt for life, and was fearfully
shot and disfigured. His skull on top and over the right eye was crushed,
probably by a rock, and there was a deep gash across his chin; the mark of
gun barrels was imprinted on his left cheek, looking as though he had
been jabbed with a gun. There were three or four buckshot wounds in his
face and head, and a pistol shot wound in the top of the left shoulder,
passing down through the trunk, probably fired when he was on his hands
and knees or after he had fallen. Holmes was shot only once, the ball
(probably from his own rifle) striking him in the left side below the arm
pit, passing through his heart and coming out at the right side, also shatter-
ing the right arm. There were no other wounds in his body. Reynolds was
found lying on his face, his overcoat and gauntlet gloves still on. Holmes,
also wearing an overcoat, lay on his back, with arms stretched out.

The Indians rifled the pockets of their victims, obtaining from Reynolds
his gold watch and chain, valued at over $200, upwards of $200 in cash,
and the key belonging to the shackles, also all the papers on his person.
The contents of Holmes' pockets is not known, but everything he had was
taken; also his hat which was picked up near the trail of the Indians, twelve
miles from the scene of killing by the citizens' posse from Globe; papers
which had been torn up and thrown away were also found. Eugene Middleton lost two coats, a watch and chain, and other articles. A shotgun, Winchester and three sixshooters, belonging to the officers, were also taken.

After the murderers had started away, one of them came back and ran
down toward Middleton, who feared it was for the purpose of giving him
the finishing shot, but the Indian passed on, without molesting him, to
where Reynolds lay, probably to get the key to the shackles which may
have been overlooked in the first search of the dead man's pockets. After
the Indians disappeared, Middleton, faint and sore walked to Riverside,
where he arrived about 7 o'clock a.m. and reported the frightful disaster.
In the meantime the Mexican, Avott, had taken one of the horses from the
team, which he mounted and as he claims, started for Florence with object
of informing the authorities of Pinal county, of the tragic occurrence. The
horse, not accustomed to being ridden, bucked him off three times, and
Avott then tied him up and continued on foot, and barefooted, to White's
ranch, where he told his story of the murder, and with the man at the ranch
went as rapidly as horses could carry them, to Florence. Sheriff Jerry Fryer,
accompanied by Pete Gabriel, Kibbey, Martin, Gibson and Miller, lost no

time in preparations for their departure from Florence and were early at the scene of killing.

D. H. Snyder and watchman at the Raymine were the first to reach the scene after the killing. They reported having found pony tracks on one side of the road and moccasin tracks on the other; also a whip stock, with blood stains upon it, from which the lash had been torn. They firmly believed that the officers had been ambushed, but there seems to be no good reason to report such an opinion. The bodies of Reynolds and Holmes were left where they fell until the afternoon of the day of the killing, when they were removed to Riverside, and an inquest held by the coroner of Pinal county.

In addition to the posse under Deputy Sheriff Ryan, there went from Globe, Mr. and Mrs. Wm. Middleton, Willis Middleton, Dr. J. W. Largent, Job Atkins, Ed. Lidlph, August Piper, and A. R. Young and Drew Fagala, who brought the bodies of Reynolds and Holmes to Globe, arriving here Sunday afternoon.

Owing to the inclement weather and the rough road over Pinal mountain to Globe, it was thought hazardous to bring Eugene Middleton home, and, accompanied by his mother he was conveyed to Florence. His condition has since greatly improved and within a few days he will be able to return to Globe. Dr. Mann, of San Carlos, at the solicitation of Mr. Wm. Middleton went to Florence to examine his son's injuries, and, if deemed necessary, to proffer his professional services. Dr. Mann found the patient mending so rapidly that he returned to San Carlos where his presence was required.

Immediately upon the receipt of news of the disaster, B. G. Fox telegraphed the meagre information to Capt. L. Johnson, commanding at San Carlos, who with commendable promptitude, notified every military post in Central and Southern Arizona—as quickly as the electric current could carry the dire tidings. As a result, within a very brief space of time, detachments of troops, under experienced officers, were in the saddle and hurrying in the direction of Riverside, or to points where the fugitive Indians might possibly be intercepted. Lieutenants Wilder and Hardeman, with 30 men from Troop G, 4th Cavalry, Lieut. Watson with 20 scouts left San Carlos at 3 P.M., Saturday, and moved rapidly toward Riverside. A detachment from Fort Thomas was among the first in the field. Troops from Forts Grant, Lowel, McDowell, Apache, and Huachuca were also quickly in the field.

Lieutenants Watson, Wilder and Hardeman took up the trail near Cunningham's ranch on the San Pedro, Sunday, and followed it eight miles beyond Dudleyville, where the Indian fugitives, hotly pressed, took to the rocks in the foot-hills of the Saddle Mountains, snow and rain interfering, the trail was lost and the progress of the troops temporarily hindered. Lieut. Watson and scouts are reported to have subsequently trailed three of the Indian escapers to Kid's camp, on the reservation. Kid and Pash-tan-tah are reported to have been seen, mounted, near the San Carlos River, four miles from the Agency, on Sunday afternoon. Lieut. Overton and troops from McDowell reached Pinal ranch on Monday, with the object of guarding the passes in that vicinity. The detachment came on to Globe on Wednesday, for instructions, and remained until Thursday morning when they departed in the direction of McMillen.

After leaving the San Pedro the trails showed that the Indians had separated and up to the present writing they have not been located.

The combined posses from Globe and Florence were the first to take up the trail, and, starting on Sunday morning, where the foul deed was committed they followed it through its various windings to within three miles of Dudleyville, where they were obliged to abandon the hunt, owing to rain which obliterated the trail, and, exhausted, they dispersed. About a mile from where the tragedy occurred, a pair of blue pants and white drawers both with blood stains upon them, were found, discarded by the Indians, and in a pocket of the pants the key of the handcuffs; papers, taken from the pockets of the officers, and torn up, were found along the trail, and about seven miles out, Holmes' hat was picked up. A carcass of a steer was also discovered, a part of which had been taken and some of the hide stripped off and used for foot covering, as evidenced by the peculiar track made by one of the fugitives after leaving the spot. After giving up the chase, Deputy Ryan and companions returned directly to Globe, arriving home Tuesday afternoon.

Brother Bennie went out to Arizona and settled up Glenn's affairs and brought his family home to Texas. There was Gustie with her four children, Elmer, Watt, Bessie and Gussie, leaving little George, who had died some time before, by his father's side in the cemetery at Globe.

The following letters show the rounds of my brother's watch from the time it was taken by his murderers to its return to his family. They also show the kindness and courtesy of the Mexican officials in returning it to his family.

Mr. Minister: Mexico, May 20th, 1890

I have the honor herewith to transmit to Your Excellency copy of communication which the Secretary of the Treasury has addressed to me, that in an encounter had by some of the Customs Guards with Apache Indians the former recovered various articles, among which was a gold watch and its chain, the property of the Sheriff of Gila County, Arizona. Said watch is in this Department subject to Your Excellency's orders, so you may send for it whenever you desire.

I renew to Your Excellency the declaration of my eminent regard.

M. ASPEROZ

Legation of the United States
Sir: Mexico, May 23, 1890

I am in receipt of Your Excellency's esteemed note of the 20th inst., informing me that a gold watch and its chain, the property of the Sheriff of Gila County, Arizona, which was recovered in a recent encounter had by Mexican Customs Guards with some Apache Indians, is now in your Department, subject to this Legation's orders.

I beg that Your Excellency will kindly cause said watch and chain to be delivered to bearer and that you will be pleased to accept this note as a receipt therefor.

Thanking Your Excellency for the kindly courtesy shown in the matter, I take pleasure in reiterating the assurance of my highest considerations of friendly esteem.

THOS. RYAN

Legation of the United States
Mexico, May 23, 1890

To the Hon. James G. Blaine
Sir: Washington, D. C.

I have the honor to forward to the Department at Washington in today's mailpouch, a gold watch and chain delivered to this Legation by the Mexican Foreign Officer, with the information that it is the property of the late Sheriff of Gila County, which was recovered in an encounter had by Mexican Customs guards with some Apache Indians. The Mexican Government with characteristic kindliness and courtesy has taken this method of returning this property to the Sheriff's family. Upon the interior case is the inscription: Glenn Reynolds, Albany, Texas, June 10th, 1884.

Copies of the correspondence relative thereto is herewith transmitted.

I am, Sir, very respectfully,   THOS. RYAN

Department of State
Washington, June 2, 1890

The Hon. Lewis Wolfley,
      Governor of Arizona
             Phoenix.
Sir:

I have the honor to transmit a copy of a dispatch from our Minister in Mexico, regarding a gold watch, the property of Mr. Glenn Reynolds, late Sheriff of Gila County, Arizona, which has been recovered by Mexican Customs Guards from Apaches. The watch will be forwarded to you by express for delivery to the rightful owner.

As the Mexican Government would be glad, no doubt, to be apprised of its receipt, I trust that such acknowledgement may be made by the recipient through your office as seems proper. I will forward the same to our Minister.

I have the honor to be, Sir, your obedient servant,

J AMES   G.   B LAINE

Gustie was soon settled in a little home in Albany and bravely took up the burden of life alone, caring for her children. Elmer, the eldest son, was twelve and being a manly little fellow was a help and comfort to his mother. We must live; life has to be faced no matter how great the loneliness and heartbreak. She was a brave Christian woman and accepted her lot with fortitude.

IV

At this time we were still living on the ranch, but in the summer I came in to town and stayed with Gustie in her little home. Here on the Second of July, our little Lucile was born, a tiny baby with brown eyes and golden curls, a little cherub. Her father was out on the ranch and was not there to welcome this baby. We had no telephones then, but he came in the next day, and looking over his new daughter critically, finally said, "Sallie, this is the 'oneriest' little baby we have had." And in the next breath he said, "Sallie, this baby looks just like you." Well, thanking him for the compliment, I did not feel the least bit cowed by the remarks; I knew he was judging by her size, not her looks. She was such a mite, but plenty big, weighing a little over five pounds. Fine goods come in small packages, you know.

The year 1892 saw us on the move again. For the sake of better school facilities and for various other reasons we decided to come back to Albany after spending four years on the ranch. We bought a small house and added some rooms, giving it a general remodeling. Then in April we moved in. It seemed rather nice to be back too, where neighbors could drop in; there is more doing than on a ranch, and we liked being with the family. As James Russell Lowell has said, "We need to be vitalized by contact with people."

In December, 1892, another link was forged between the two families. This time it was Frazier Cantelou, grandnephew of my mother, and Lula Matthews, who had been reared in the home of Brother George since she was nine years of age. She had a lovely wedding in their home. They went to Oklahoma City to live where Frazier had a position in the First National Bank which had been organized there by Brother George and others in the beginning of the boom when Oklahoma City consisted of a few wooden shacks. J. P. Boyle, who had married Vallie Wilson, cousin of the Matthews, was in charge of this bank at the time.

This year, 1892, John bought Mr. Sam Webb's interest in the real estate and insurance firm of Webb & Hill which had been in business here many years. Mr. Webb went to Waco to take over the management of the banking business of his father-in-law, Mr. Taylor, who had recently died. Real estate and insurance was a new departure for a cattleman, one who had been raised on the wide prairies and knew the cattle business from start to finish but little of any other business. However, a good part of this work was not unfamiliar to him for in making loans, land had to be inspected and passed upon and he was an old hand at that.

The firm of Hill & Matthews continued for only a short time, a year or so, when John sold out to Mr. Webb, who had lived in this country too long and had to come back. The firm became Webb & Hill again. About this time they took Thomas L. Blanton, a nephew of Mr. Webb, into the firm as attorney.

v

In the summer of 1893 a party of us went up to Chicago to attend the World's Columbian Exposition. We rented one of the new apartments that had been built to accommodate visitors to the fair. Ours was a very commodious one on Prairie Avenue, and we needed a big one for we were a large party; there were William and Susie, with three children, Eaton, Ella, and Merle, I, with May, Joe, Susette and Baby Sallie, our sixth little girl, and a nurse. We went up the first of July and spent the month; part of us were there a full month. Sister and her daughter, May, spent two weeks and went on to Bristol, Connecticut, to finish the summer. Brother George, Sister Bettie and Elmer Reynolds, a nephew, went to South Dakota where Reynolds Brothers had a ranch. John came up later with his sister, Mattie, and her daughter, Carrie.

We really had a rollicking good time. The children thoroughly enjoyed seeing the city as well as the exposition, as did we all. We were duly impressed by the court of honor, flanked on either side by the white classic buildings, and the men and boys especially enjoyed the exhibits in the Transportation Building.

Before we were to leave for home Sallie took sick. She was very ill for a day or so and I was extremely anxious to get her home to our own doctor, so as soon as she was well enough to move we started for home and she improved all the way down.

There were many babies at the fair; the nursery or *creche* at the fair grounds was running over with them. There were two mothers with babies on our Pullman going up who had no nurses with them. I asked one of them if she were going to leave her baby in the nursery. She clasped him to her breast and said, "No, I do not think I can leave my baby in the nursery." The next morning when we reached the fair grounds we stopped by the nursery and met these two women coming out; they had both left their babies.

VI

The next year John announced that he was going to run for the office of county judge. The commissioners' court had threatened to raise the taxes, that is, to render the land for more than it was worth. They were holding hearings, and on being called before them, John said that they should cut the pattern to fit the cloth, that if they could not run on the money that came in, they should get out. They suggested that he show them how; hence, his decision. When he told me he was going to run, I did not like the idea, and asked him why he had decided to do that. He replied that he wanted to get rid of his nickname, "Bud." He was elected and served two terms at the huge salary of fifty dollars a month, during which taxes, instead of being raised, were lowered. After his second term he was quite satisfied and did not run again.

He forever lost his name of "Bud" and is known far and near as "Judge Matthews," except by a few of his oldtime friends who still call him "Bud," and there are so few left. Believe me, I think that old boyhood name sounds rather sweet to him now when someone affectionately says "Bud."

On December 15, 1894, we welcomed our second boy, J. A., Jr. After four little girls all in a row, this little boy was of course a delight to his father's heart, which is no reflection on girls. It is nice to have both. While the children are coming and in their babyhood, I must admit that the road seems rough and hard to travel at times; nursing them through the ills of childhood and caring for them by day and by night is a wearisome task. Any mother of a large family certainly earns her salt as she goes along if she does her duty by her family, but how richly repaid we are if they grow up into honorable men and women, and what an untold pleasure along the way.

VII

On the Twenty-fifth of June, 1895, occurred the most disastrous hail storm ever known in this country, and I dare say no country has a parallel to this terrific storm. It came almost without warning; chunks of ice suddenly began falling, knocking up dust. My husband, Dave Campbell and one of his boys, and John Matthews, a cousin, were driving in from the ranch. They soon saw that they must find shelter, and turning into Mr. Lipscomb's place on the outskirts of Albany, they drove into his yard, loosened their horses from the buggy as quickly as possible and ran into the house, while the horses, which would have followed if they could, crowded against the lea side of the house as closely as they could for protection. Rain came in torrents and hail in huge chunks, and I still remember the feeling of awe I had while this terrific battle of the elements was raging. Split shingles from the roof were flying in all directions, window glass splintering, and in at least one instance an immense hailstone came through both roof and ceiling and into the room. This storm lasted only a short time; if it had been of long duration there would have been little of Albany left. As it was, there were few if any whole windows left on the northwest side of the houses, weatherboarding was knocked off and roofs were battered to pieces.

VIII

On the Twenty-seventh of June, 1895, dear Father Matthews died suddenly of an attack of angina pectoris. The following are paragraphs from an article written by N. H. Burns, one of his many friends:

Uncle Joe was a man of very strong character, independent in his opinions and unyielding in his convictions, a man of generous impulses and a warm and attached friend. He was brave, and it mattered not whether he was engaged on the frontier in protecting the women and children from the tomahawk and scalping knife, or in upholding the weak against those who would oppress them, he exhibited at all times that spirit that is only to be found in heroes. In his business relations he was just, and in his charities he was liberal and sympathetic. His life was an example of industry, energy, integrity, faithfulness to trusts, justice: all the manly virtues.

He was ever ready and willing to give advice to those in trouble, and no man or woman ever lived in a community who was called on so often as a mediator and advisor, who combined all the qualities of a natural-born peacemaker to a greater extent than was possessed by him. The children all loved him and considered him a second father.

In turning the pages of my memory I can recall nothing in the history of man that can parallel this universal popularity, and he is the one man of whom I can truly say I never have heard an unkind word spoken.—One who loved him.

IX

Now some of the children thought they would like to learn something of stringed instruments, so we obtained a teacher, Miss Odelia Reisner, now Mrs. H. T. Staiti of Houston. Miss Ottie, as she was called, was a charming addition to Albany society and to our church as she had a fine singing voice, which is always so welcome in a choir. Joe and all our girls studied music under her. This was kept up for two years and there was a lot of pleasure along with the two years of music. The young people and their elders enjoyed it all.

In thinking of these bygone days, how we were struggling and bending every effort for the benefit of our children's education and culture, trying to furnish them privileges that we in our pioneer upbringing had been denied, I am reminded of something my dear old mother, sitting quietly by, observing with her keen mind all that was going on, said to me one day. "Sallie, if your children are not a whole lot better and a whole lot smarter than you are, there is lots of time and money wasted on them."

Now our children were reaching the age to go away to school. Seven of these cousins and double cousins, including our May and Joe, went to the San Antonio Academy at the same time. They did good work in this school and enjoyed San Antonio. Other cousins went to other schools.

After sending so many of our children away, it occurred to us to build an academy of our own and keep our children at home. I think this idea emanated from Mr. French McAfee, our pastor, who also fostered and encouraged the idea of building a new church. Our little wooden church, the first to be built in Albany, was looking old and shabby; besides, it was small for this ever growing and increasing generation of young people. This idea of building began to work lively and soon plans were on foot to build a new church and academy. An architect was employed to draw plans, contracts were let, and workmen began on both buildings about the same time. All this delighted the soul of our pastor, and he was about the busiest and happiest man in town as he went from one to the other of the buildings that were going up.

In September, even though the academy was not finished, a faculty was brought together and the school was opened, part of it being taught in a vacated store building on Main Street and the primary classes being held in the church.

Work progressed on the two buildings and on January 10, 1898, the Reynolds Presbyterian Academy, named in honor of my father, was opened. It was a beautiful building of pressed brick

REYNOLDS PRESBYTERIAN ACADEMY,
*named for Barber Watkins Reynolds, was completed in 1898. It
later became Reynolds Presbyterian Orphanage. After removal of
the Orphanage to Dallas, the building was razed in 1927.*

MATTHEWS MEMORIAL PRESBYTERIAN CHURCH,
*located in Albany, was built in 1898. Dedicated to Joseph Beck
Matthews, it became Sallie Reynolds Matthews's family church.*

with trim of white stone, modern in every way and well equipped. A music room had a good piano, the library room had already quite a stock of books, two sets of encyclopedias and many of the English classics. There was everything that could be thought of to encourage and inspire children that they might aspire to the high and noble things of life. The building was a credit to the citizens of Albany who were interested and had helped with their means. All were proud of the handsome building on the hill just west of town. There was an agreement among Brother George, Brother Will and John that they would for five years pay any deficiency that might occur in running the school. In other words, if it should not be self-supporting, they would come to the rescue.

Although we had this fine school here, that did not seem to satisfy very long. Soon we were sending children away to other schools. Some were sent to Roswell Military Academy at Roswell, New Mexico, some, including our son, Joe, went to Austin college in Sherman, and others went to the New England Conservatory of Music in Boston. Our daughter, Susette, went to Hardin College in Missouri and afterward to the Conservatory in Boston.

I think perhaps the idea had been that there were too many of one family in the Reynolds Academy to do good work and that it might be better to separate them; however, we did send them off to school in groups. I want to make it plain, as there might be a wrong impression drawn from these last remarks, that there was very little disagreeing among themselves. I look back upon those times when that host of girls and boys, first cousins, double first cousins and near double first cousins, were growing up in this little village, and I marvel at the smooth, amicable way in which they got along. They loved each other devotedly and would stand together to the last ditch. Of course they had their squabbles, but they were few and small. It was just that they had such a good time together, in school or out of school, morning, noon and night, that it was hard for them to apply themselves to their school work as they should. When we are living things we cannot appreciate the situation as we do in retrospect. The way in which those youngsters got along together seems marvelous to me now.

The academy, which had been raised to the rank of a college, after ten or twelve years of service was finally abandoned for want of patronage. It seemed sad that after such an auspicious beginning it should end in this way. Even so, it served a good purpose in raising a standard for higher education in this part of the country and it was a great benefit to the general public. No good work is ever lost and this school did good work, and instilled higher ambitions in the bosoms of some which perhaps would not have been gained otherwise.

The Reynolds Presbyterian Orphanage took the place of the academy, under the supervision of Mr. and Mrs. J. Gilmore Smith, under whose regime it prospered for several years before being moved to Dallas where it is now.

x

Now comes our third little boy and last child. He was called Watt, his full name being Watkins Reynolds Matthews for my father.

At this time the new church was almost finished, a splendid building of solid, native stone. In April, 1899, the Matthews Memorial Church was dedicated to the worship of God, in memory of Father Matthews ("Uncle Joe"). The dedicatory sermon was delivered by Dr. Little, our synodical evangelist, Mr. McAfee being host. It was a beautiful and impressive service and we were all proud of the lovely building.

Soon after the completion of the church, our beloved pastor decided his work in Albany was done and he resigned his pastorate to our sorrow. We did not want him to leave but he thought best to go. He had been the inspiration behind the building of the new church and academy, and had reason to be proud of the work he had done in Albany in many ways. His teaching and preaching were an inspiration and an uplift.

The first wedding in the new church was that of our eldest daughter, May, on the 27th of September, 1899. I shall quote here the first paragraph from an article in our town paper:

> One of the picture weddings one is privileged occasionally to attend, occurred in Matthews Memorial Church, Albany, Texas, when Miss May Louise Matthews, eldest daughter of Judge and Mrs. J. A. Matthews, was married to Mr. Thomas Lindsay Blanton, the unusually promising young lawyer of the late law firm of Blanton & Hill.

May Bartholomew sang *Oh Promise Me* as the bridal party entered, and as it withdrew after the ceremony performed by Mr. McAfee, the loved strains of Mendelssohn's *Wedding March* swelled and filled the building. Immediately after, there was a reception at our home.

So the closing year of the century was marked for us by the birth of our last child and the marriage of our eldest.

Gateway, Lambshead Ranch — Established 1897.

*Ruins of the George T. Reynolds
house, destroyed by fire in 1931.*

Addenda

‹‹

A JOURNAL OF A TRIP FROM THE CLEAR FORK IN STEPHENS COUNTY TO THE SAN SABA RIVER

by SAM P. NEWCOMB

ON THE 1st of February, 1864, we, seven in number, left B. W. Reynolds' Ranch on Clear Fork of Brazos, about 5 o'clock P.M. The weather is warm and clear. We have two pack horses, packed with over two hundred pounds of flour, and some bacon, salt, etc.; we ate supper at the mouth of Snakeden on the Clear Fork, and struck camp No. 1 about two miles from the river, where we hoppled our horses and built a good fire. No camp yarns spun of much interest, as the boys have not gotten very well acquainted yet.

Muster Roll of the Party

George T. Reynolds	William Herall	Levi Shaw
Holl Clark	Sam Newcomb	Tom Smith
		Tom Fitch

Feb. 2nd. This morning we were aroused from our slumbers by Sharp Pistol Tom (Fitch) at the break of day. As there was no water near we saddled, and packed up, and rode for Hubbard Creek for our breakfast; we struck the creek in the Negro Valley and there we ate our breakfast and dinner in the same meal. Here Sharp Pistol Tom concluded it was not worth while to wash, but the boys said so much about it that he changed his mind and washed for FEAR, as he said, that some of them would get mad about it. After resting ourselves about two hours, we took up our line of march and about 4 o'clock P.M., we came to the Snalum Ranch, where we met with some of our neighbors from the Clear Fork hunting beef. After a great deal of contrariness and disputing we camped with the beef hunters on Hubbard about a half mile from the Ranch. This was camp No. 2. The subject of organizing the county into a company and forting up, was well debated upon. We also got a full description of the MUSK HOG from Mr. Irwin.

Feb. 3rd. We awoke rather early this morning and commenced cooking breakfast as our cooked supplies had given out. William and Sharp Pistol Tom took some flour to the Ranch to get it cooked, while the rest of the boys caught up the horses and came on. Our horses having been on better grass than usual, girted a little more. We struck that prong of Hubbard called Deep Creek three miles from where we camped and ate dinner, as we would not get any more water until night. We traveled up the divide of Hubbard and Deep creek, seeing but little game, a few deer and antelope. About noon we grazed our horses on good grass. After resting two or three hours we took up our line of march, and soon crossed an old government road running from Camp Cooper. Just as the sun was setting we camped on Deep Creek about ten miles below Bob Sloan's Ranch No. 3.

Feb. 4th.   When we awoke this morning the sun had driven away the darkness of night and was not long in making its appearance. We had some trouble in finding our horses this morning; they had strolled a long way from camp. We kept up the creek passing Sloan's Ranch where we borrowed a cup from Mrs. Breuer, as we had only one canteen to carry water in. About three miles up the creek, we passed another Ranch where we got directions to the Colorado River, and also heard that an Indian had come in and given himself up to a ranch in that neighborhood a few days before. We struck camp No. 4 at the last water on the right hand prong of the creek about 12 o'clock, where we stayed till the next day. Having no meat but bacon, we killed an unmarked yearling for fresh eating. Weather still pleasant.

Feb. 5th.   This morning we took our course about due South and passed over the ridge between Deep Creek and Pecan Bayou; we saw a few antelope to-day; Sam shot at one; Tom S. broke one's hind leg, and Levi broke one's fore legs and caught it by hard running. We nooned on the main prong of P. B. and struck camp No. 5 on the main prong about 4 o'clock. We were troubled to find water that we could drink, as there was but little, and it full of dead fish. There are plenty of pecans on the creek.

Feb. 6th.   This morning the wind was blowing rather cold from the North. We took our course for the Post Oak Mountains. There is a great deal of timber on these mountains, and plenty of deer. George succeeded in killing one. Just South of these mountains we took the old Fort Chadburn and Camp Colorado road which is very dim. We ate dinner at a small mudhole where the boys discovered a buffalo about a half mile off, and Levi, Holl and Tom S. started to give him battle. They took a branch on him and Tom S. gave him a deadly shot. From there we went to what we supposed to be Jim Ned, and struck camp No. 6. Here we started another buffalo and set our dog Caesar on it. He caught and stopped it so the boys could kill it. We have seen several prairie dog towns to-day. They were new and not very large.

Feb. 7th. This being Sunday and our horses poor we stayed at camp No. 6. There was some ice this morning, but it proved to be a warm and pleasant day. Nothing of interest took place to-day, except a few bluffs at wrestling and a few foot races were run.

Feb. 8th. Monday. This morning early we were on our way, but Sharp Pistol Tom missed his powder horn which hindered us some. Deer and antelope were plentiful to-day but none killed. Our party got separated to-day through sap-headed contrariness and the result was a serious fight came very near taking place. We traveled hard all day without water for ourselves or our horses. About sundown we crossed a road that had the appearance of being traveled considerable; soon after we came to a small creek running a little west of south where we found a hole of green water, full of dead turtles, very large ones; our horses drank heartily but we could not taste it, dry as we were. We followed the creek down until very late in the night, when we at last found a very nice pool of good water. After cooking and eating our supper we retired to our camp pallets No. 7.

Feb. 9th. Weather fine and game plenty. Sam and Sharp Pistol Tom killed an antelope apiece, Tom Smith killed a deer. We passed through a great many prairie dog towns and Levi succeeded in killing one, Bill killed a yearling, so we have plenty of beef as long as it will last. About 12 o'clock we struck the Colorado River; after tracing it down a few miles we struck camp No. 8. Weather fair.

Feb. 10th. This morning we started for the mouth of Concho, down the Colorado. On our way we met up with six men from Palo Pinto County, hunting stock ranches. We ate dinner with Messers McCane and Hunter, who have settled on the Concho about two miles from the mouth. The Concho is a beautiful stream of water but has very little timber on it, and the grass is not of the best quality. Prairie dog towns very plentiful. We struck camp No. 9 about 10 miles above the mouth of Concho. Pecans appear to have been quite plentiful.

Feb. 11th. The weather this morning is warm and has the appearance of rain, we traveled up the Concho, and soon after starting jumped an old buffalo cow, which was killed by Sam. We struck camp No. 10 on Concho, about 3 miles above the mouth of Kickapoo creek. To-day we saw a few swan and one was killed by Sam. After striking camp, Tom S. and Sam went out to look for game, but got nothing but a wetting, for it commenced raining soon after dark but did not rain much.

Feb. 12th.   This morning we took our course about South for the Kickapoe Springs, about 12 o'clock we came in sight of seven Indians, driving
ninety head of horses. We unloaded our pack horses and gave them a chase.
They caught fresh horses out of the herd and tried hard to out-run us but
they had too large a drove. They gave them up without a word and rode
off. Besides the horses we picked up one good saddle, one well dressed
buffalo skin, two canteens, three pairs of moccasins and some other small
tricks. We drove the horses back the trail until dark and then kept the
course as well as we could until about ten o'clock, when we stopped and
guarded them with our horses saddled all night. This camp No. 11; we
camped without fire or water. Weather cool.

Feb. 13th.   At the break of day we started our captured horses for the
settlements to find their owners. Ten o'clock A.M. we came to water and
cooked the first meal for the last thirty hours. It rained on us a little in the
evening. We stopped after dark on a branch and struck camp No. 12, under
projecting cliff of rocks, a very good retreat from the rain. The latter part
of the night was very dark, so dark we could not see to guard our horses.

Feb. 14th.   In the morning we found our stock very badly scattered,
but think we got them all. We kept down the creek until we came to the
San Saba River where we soon found settlements. We have stopped for
the present at Mr. Jackson's. This evening some of the boys caught an
unbroke horse to ride. We struck camp No. 13 in Mr. Jackson's blacksmith
shop.

Feb. 15th.   Learning that we had a mare belonging to Mr. Fields, who
lives about twelve miles up the river, Sam and Tom S. accompanied by
old man Tucker, went to see him about it. They returned at sundown with
Mr. Fields. This morning Mrs. Tucker took our dirty clothes to the wash
and she not only washed but mended them nicely. Still camped in the old
shop—weather fair.

Feb. 16th.   This morning Mr. Fields took his mare off of our hands,
after paying us $30 for her (Confederate money). We bought 18 pounds
of bacon of Mr. Jackson and moved our horses four miles down the river
to Mr. Casey's. We left two wounded horses with Mr. J. and a colt with
Mrs. Tucker. We struck camp No. 14 in Mr. Casey's pens with our horses.
Tom S. swapped horses to-day with Mr. Fields and thinks he made a good
trade.

Feb. 17th.   The weather is still fine. We heard where some of our horses
belonged to-day. Levi and Fitch worked at some larrietts to-day while the

rest of the boys herded horses. We are treated very friendly by Mr. Casey and family, and many other.

Feb. 18th. This morning the wind was blowing very cold and fresh from the north; so cold that we did not take our horses out until about noon. We have partly broken four or five young horses which we intend to keep. At the setting of the sun the wind lay, and the night was more pleasant than the day had been.

Feb. 19th. After breakfast Bill and Sam started down the country to find the owners of our captured property. When within 15 miles of Fort Mason they met two gentlemen coming up to look at the horses. They learned from them that there was good grass in about six miles from Mason, so they sent the boys word to bring the horses down. They camped at a spring on Honey creek. Grass very good.

Feb. 20th. As soon as it was light, Sam and Bill saddled their stock and rode over to Mr. Lindsey's on Comanche creek and ate breakfast with his step-son-in-law, where they had old-fashioned coffee. After breakfast they went to Mason with Mr. L. and his step-son-in-law. There were a few people in town, mostly Dutch. It was tax paying day, and Mr. Todd was trying to organize a company but it appeared to be a dull business. Fort Mason is situated on a very high, dry and rocky hill; on the north side of the hill and about five hundred yards from the Post, is a bold and beautiful spring the only water near the place. The country around for a few miles looks dry and there is no grass nor water for stock. Bill and Sam went back to Honey Spring and camped at the same place they did the night before. Weather still pleasant.

Feb. 21st. This morning Bill and Sam started back to the horses having heard that the boys were not coming down with them. A few men have called to look at them, one, L. Taylor, had a horse lariatted to see if it was his, and broke its neck. The boys often get out of soap, and as they sit around the campfire, Bill sometimes revives their dull spirits by imitating some ladies and gents as they dance at parties in Stephens county. To-night Bill talked Dutch for the boys as he had paid particular attention to some Dutch talking in Fort Mason. He gave us a lengthy description of the Dutch, and a little smattering of their language.

Feb. 22nd. We drove the horses to Honey creek and struck camp No. 15 at the Spring on the head of the creek. Here we have good grass but not much water for horses. We will herd to-night, as they have not grazed much to-day. Weather fair and warm.

Feb. 23rd.   We think of stopping where we are, as we have good grass and can get more water with a little labor; two horses were taken off our hands to-day, Mr. Merrell took his after a great deal of growling about our charges and expressed his satisfaction that we did not have the other one as he would not be able to pay for her. Such being the case, we were as glad as he was. A little gambling was carried on by visitors by way of horse racing and pulling straws. We drove our horses to Mr. Lindsey's pen last night and struck camp No. 16. Still very dry.

Feb. 24th.   We drove back to Honey creek this morning and concluded to herd them there day and night. Levi and Tom S. went to the San Saba Ranger camp to see if they could get any gun caps, tobacco, etc. They got a little tobacco but no caps. The Captain sent us word to bring the horses in to their camp and offered assistance in taking care of them, but we concluded not to go. About sundown it looked like rain but it failed to come. We struck camp No. 17 near Honey Springs.

Feb. 25th.   We butchered a beef to-day as we were entirely out of meat. Weather begins to have the appearance of Spring but is very dry.

Feb. 26th.   This morning two of the boys went to Fort Mason to buy bread stuff, the rest were busily engaged in herding and making larietts; while thus engaged we were taken by surprise by Lieutenant McDowell with 20 men from camp San Saba. He had strict orders from Captain O'Brine to arrest and bring us and our horses to camp without fail. We were outnumbered, so we were compelled to obey the foolish order, caused by some scandalous and malicious falsehoods told by envious scamps, without principle or honor. We got to camp about sundown and were received very friendly by Captain O'Brine; we were shown an old cabin that we might occupy; here we struck camp No. 18.

Feb. 27th.   This morning Sam had an interview with the Capt. concerning our arrest. His excuse was, that on the day we proposed to sell the horses, the Rangers could not be at the sale, as on that day (March 1st.) they were to be transferred to the Confederate service. Grass around camp very short. Camp San Saba has a pretty situation on the San Saba River near the mouth of Tecumseh creek; there are in the camp about 15 families.

Feb. 28th.   This is Sunday and a very cold norther blowing, made worse by a cold rain, but the rain is very much needed. We did not help herd to-day as we were considered prisoners.

Feb. 29th.   Very cold, hail and sleet.

Mar. 1st.   Very cold, ground covered with snow but very pleasant over head. Before night the snow had disappeared, and nothing was left to show that we had had a cold snow storm.

Mar. 2nd.   This morning we were expecting to start back to the Kickapoe Springs, but the officers were opposed to us taking a horse apiece. We agreed to leave it to two or three disinterested citizens, but could not find any that would agree to arbitrate the question for us.

Mar. 3rd.   Finding it useless to try to get anything for our trouble, out of the horses, we saddled our own broken down ones, some of which had to be helped up when they were down, and started back home. We traveled very slow as we had to walk part of the time, and some of us all the time. We ate supper at a spring between San Saba and Mr. Lindsey's. After dark we rode about a mile west to find grass where we stopped for camp No. 19. While we were at camp San Saba we were treated very friendly by some and by others the reverse. Capt. Cooch, Steve Caveness, Dick Nelson, Jem Tannee and a few others treated us like men, but—Clark, Tink Mabery,—Middleton and others, acted a conspicuous part in trying to do us all the harm in their power.

Mar. 4th.   This morning we found a cold damp norther blowing from the cold yankee regions. As we had no water near we took up our line of march for the Honey Springs for breakfast, Sam went by Mr. Lindsey's to look for his pocket compass which he had lost a week before. About 12 o'clock he met the boys at the spring. He found his compass and also a box of matches which he lost at the same time. Here we grazed our horses until dark. Just after dark we saddled and rode a mile to good grass and rolled in for camp No. 20.

Mar. 5th.   We struck the Mason and Fort McKavett road soon after we started, and left it within two or three miles of Pegleg, there we turned down a branch and soon after found water, where we ate supper and struck camp No. 21. Our horses being so poor we concluded to stay here a few days, as we have very good water, grass, plenty of wood and a good shelter if it should storm. Most of our party are anxious to get home, but all deny being homesick.

Mar. 6th.   Levi is a little unwell to-day but do not think him dangerous. This is Sunday, but the boys amused themselves by pitching dollars. In the evening Sharp Pistol Tom complained of something like an ague. After talking of home, our wives and sweet-hearts, our courtships, etc., we retired to our camp pallets, and dreamed of all the love, sweetness and pleasures of home, in blissful visions. No rain yet.

Mar. 7th.   This day makes five weeks since we left home, or have slept in a bed. We are looked for every day by this time, and here we are yet, two hundred miles from home. Wives and sweet-hearts will look with tearfully anxious eyes, for several long days before we return. Weather still pleasant and dry. The boys pass the time in telling stories and making fun in various ways.

Mar. 8th.   At daybreak the sky was cloudy, but it soon cleared off pleasant. We took our march up the Fort Mason and McKavett road, passing Pegleg and Mr. Casey's Ranch at noon; we came to Mr. Jackson's and settled a bacon debt with him, and took dinner with the friendly Mrs. Tucker; we struck camp No. 22 on the south bank of San Saba River one mile below the old Spanish Fort. At this place some of the boys caught a few nice fish. After dark there came up a thunder shower but it did not give us much of a washing, nothing like what we needed.

Mar. 9th.   After breakfast Sharp Pistol Tom, Levi and Tom S. took the pack horses and kept up the road while the rest of us crossed over to the north side of the river to look at the old Spanish Fort. This Fort is on the north bank of the San Saba River about 20 miles below McKavett. We were not able to learn much of its history, but it has the appearance of being built a great many years ago. It is more than a hundred yards square, built of large rock; the walls must have been 20 feet high or more, and are double, standing 6 or 8 feet apart, making a space of this width between the walls, all the way around the Fort. This wall is divided into rooms by rock partitions and have the appearance of having been covered with flat dirt roofs. In the northwest corner are the largest buildings, all of rock which may have been the commissary or the quarters of the principal officers. Also in the southwest and southeast corners there have been large rock buildings, but not so large and strong as the others. In these buildings remain some of the fireplaces and doorways leading from room to room, and large vaults left in the wall, which puzzled the mind to imagine for what use they were put to. Near the largest buildings on the west is the only gateway leading into the Fort. On the righthand side of the gate going in is written ARCOS PADILLA 1810, and other Spanish and English dates and names so old that we could not make them out. Just outside the enclosure, on the northwest corner, is a mound which has the appearance of having been a magazine under ground. In the Fort are three or four holes that look like wells, almost filled up, and large mesquite and hackberry that have grown up and died in the buildings, since the Fort was evacuated. About 500 yards below is the Sallugg, a beautiful clear running stream. All traces of a road have been washed away and grown over. On the opposite side of the river are ditches where they irrigated a large valley. The only story we can learn is a winding up sketch of its history which is about as follows. The Mexicans or Spaniards held it in possession and were working silver mines in the neighborhood around it; they sent a hundred men after provisions and they never returned. They then sent out two hundred men and they shared the same fate. The Fort was then besieged by Indians, and starved out. And when they were past making any resistance the Indians scaled the walls and not a man escaped, except one who was out horse hunting and a woman who was down on the river. These only were saved to tell the tale. Whether this is true or not we cannot say. We traveled up San Saba River and ate dinner on Clear Creek. Here we met a man by the name of Wills making improvements. We struck camp No. 23 on the San Saba about a mile above the mouth of Clear Creek. Sharp Pistol Tom and Tom S. went up to the settlement on the head of the creek, which is only two miles from its mouth. At bedtime they came back with Mr. Johnson from McKane's Ranch. They also had some bacon and a turkey, which the kind people had given them.

Mar. 10th. Weather cool. After breakfast we went to the settlement and concluded to stay a day or two to let our horses recruit a little. We struck camp No. 24 at the fountain head of a creek which is a large spring, it is about forty steps long and runs with a rushing noise. The people have a large dam built across the stream about 400 yards below the spring which will irrigate a great deal of land. The people here appear very kind-hearted and treat us very friendly.

Mar. 11th. To-day we borrowed a washing outfit and gave our clothes a scrubbing. As most of us did not have but one suit we had to wash part at a time, some were in their drawers without pants and some in pants without drawers, some in their coats without shirts, and one way and some another, some dressed and some not at all. Some of the boys complain of severe colds that almost run to the ague; weather pleasant.

Mar. 12th. The people are very kind to us for strangers. They gave us provisions and we could not persuade them to take pay. After breakfast we bade them farewell and took up our line of march up the San Saba River to Fort McKavett, which is near the head of this stream. The country affords good range, but good timber is very scarce. Live Oak and Mesquite are the principal growth on the uplands. We struck camp No. 25 on the north bank of the river, opposite the Fort. The citizens are trying to irrigate two or three tracts of land with wheels. There are seven or eight families in and around the Fort. We met with a Mr. Kemp, an acquaintance of Mr. Johnson, the new member of our party. Mr. Kemp tried to get up a dance in the Fort but it was an entire failure except a little stag dance. Young ladies were not plentiful enough and married ones did not like to dance. They have a nice place to dance in the Colonel's quarters which is a very large and fine house. Tom S. was very sick to-night with fever and ague.

Mar. 13th. This is Sunday and a cold norther blowing. As Tom is not well we will remain in camp. This evening it looked so much like rain that all the party except George and Sharp Pistol Tom went up into the Fort and slept in the Colonel's quarters.

Mar. 14th. Instead of rain the weather is still colder. Tom S. is no better, not able to ride. Three of our party, George, Levi and Sharp Pistol Tom, not willing to wait, started for the Kickapoo this morning. We doctored Tom S. pretty freely with button willow tea for chills. He laid on his pallet and made a pretty good horse trade to-day, the second since he left home. Our new friend Johnson got a bucket full of nicely cooked biscuits of Mrs. Champee to eat while on our way to the springs.

Mar. 15th. This morning was still very cold but Tom being better we started for the springs. There is an old government road leading from McKavett past the springs and on to Fort Chadburn. The country between San Saba and Kickapoo is uneven but not rough. The range is very good mesquite; the principal timber is live oak with some mesquite. We arrived at the springs a little before sundown and found six men already building at our selected place; we also found our party that preceded us, camped at the spring, No. 26. This spring is a very pretty, bold running fountain head. It is not as large as Clear Springs but situated in a prettier place. All the news of interest the boys had to tell us was of a notorious MUSK HOG FIGHT. The contending armies were George and Levi and our dog Caesar on one side and about ten musk hogs on the other. Both armies would rallie, charge and then retreat, first one and then the other. I believe the musk hog army got the worst of the battle; their loss was one killed and three wounded. The other army came out a little better only one wounded, unless it was making retreats in disorder. The weather is very cold, had a little snow to-day.

Mar. 16th. Weather pleasant to-day but nights are very cool. The boys scattered out to-day to look at the country and find locations for stock ranches. The range is very good; the general appearance of the country is uneven but not very rough, with a few scattering mesquite and live oak;

the creek runs nicely a few miles, then sinks and stands in holes for a few miles; there is some very good burr oak timber in the bottoms and some other kinds; there is some land along the creek that could be irrigated by dams and elevators. A few musk hog fights came off to-day but they are too common to raise much of an excitement now that we have all seen them.

Mar. 17th.   There are some deer in the country, Sharp Pistol Tom killed a fine buck to-day. Sam has selected a location and commenced getting out board timber; Tom S. laid a claim at the Springs which consists of a fish and two poles. There is a great deal of beaver sign along the creek, some very large dams. Bob and Sam made a special trade to-day in boots and shoes.

Mar. 18th.   Bill, Bob, Holl and Sharp Pistol Tom started down the creek in search of a beef and expected to be gone two days. About bed time we were surprised by the hunters driving up a drove of cattle and commenced shooting; after shooting six times they succeeded in bringing one to the ground, which was doing very well considering it was dark. They butchered and hung it up which took 'till midnight; weather fair; Holl was quite unwell to-day; Tom S., George and Bill are all on the sick list. Some of the boys have rigged their saddles in a hostile manner with musk hog skins.

Mar. 19th.   To-day Sam planted a little garden of pepper, gourds, tobacco, onions, etc., which was probably the first work in the agricultural line that was ever done on Kickapoo creek. Two of our boys, Bill and Sharp Pistol Tom, and three of the other party who are improving at the Springs, started for the Lapan Spring about noon to-day. The horses belonging to George and Tom are missing to-day. Weather fine.

Mar. 20th.   This morning George and Holl went back towards McKavett in search of the missing horses. Soon after 12 o'clock the party that went to Lapan returned to camp; they say it is a pretty country with live oak ridges; range thick and good; the creek a running stream not as large as Kickapoo; building timber very scarce. We have barbecued some of our beef and will dry the balance; sky cloudy.

Mar. 21st.   This morning before day it commenced to rain, thundered and lightened like it was going to give us a good shower. We took up our pallets and went over to our neighbors and got under their house that they had got covered, but it failed to rain much. Soon after sunrise it cleared up and we went to our work. About one o'clock P.M. the hunters returned with their runaway horses, alright. In the evening it looked so much like rain that we camped with our neighbors.

Mar. 22nd.   Our neighbors finished their work to-day, and took a farewell musk hog hunt. This evening we borrowed a wagon and hauled some logs and poles. Tom S. has succeeded in sowing his tobacco seed, which required more industry than common people are endowed with, we all know.

Mar. 23rd. Our neighbors left for home to-day, and we took possession of their house which was covered but not walled. Sam added corn, peas, radishes and melons to his garden. Holl laid the foundation of a cabin about the size of a hen house to hold his claim for a stock ranch. About dark it began to rain and continued till midnight.

Mar. 24th. We were aroused before day from our peaceful slumbers by Tom S. attempting to bake his first loaf of bread. The loaf must have been unmanagable, by the cursing it got, but when it was done it would have made the Queen's cook grin to have seen it. We will make no attempt to describe it, as it is entirely out of our descriptive powers. Bill remarked that the builder of that loaf of bread ought to cook one more and then start for the country where brimstone is so plentiful and water so scarce. Tom S. replied, yes, and take you along with him. South wind all day; some of the boys went hunting but brought nothing in.

Mar. 25th. Weather pleasant again. The boys brought in seven musk hog hides to-day. Levi and Bob traded pantaloons to-day. Levi gave his buckskins for Bob's jeans and some boot. Levi and George have some pet squirrels which they think a great deal of, and intend taking them home.

Mar. 26th. Some of the boys killed a musk hog to-day, and Sam finished fencing his land. Bill and Sam made a spur trade, and Bob sold Tom S. his buckskin pants which came a little below Tom's knees just far enough to leave a broad strip of naked skin between his pants and socks. Weather pleasant.

Mar. 27th. Sunday, and the wind blowing hard from the west. The day was put in making rawhide quirts and larietts. We expect to start home in the morning and are anxiously waiting for the morning to come. The Col. has stayed about as long as he wished to, altogether he did not expect when he left home to get to stay as long as he would like. Holl goes by the name of colonel since he got a new old hat at McKavett, and the boys burned his old one up.

Mar. 28th. This morning bright and early we started for that sweet place to the traveler called home. Our horses have improved some since we have been at the Springs. Bill and Bob are going to stay; they rode with us a few miles, and then we bid our old friend Bill goodbye, until we meet again, if ever. We took the old McKavett and Chadburn road

which leads down Kickapoo, across Concho and Colorado. In the evening
we found sign where the Indians had taken out a large drove of horses.
About four o'clock P.M. we struck camp No. 27 on Concho at the Paint
Bluff. There are a great many Indian paintings on this bluff, of more shapes
imaginable, and names of many visitors. Our supplies consist of three
quarts of corn meal, so we killed a beef; after eating an Indian bate of
beef we rolled into our pallets.

Mar. 29.   Soon after sunrise we were on our way bound for home via
old Fort Chadburn. The country between Concho and Colorado is level
and covered with dog towns. We saw a few wild horses and some buffalo
to-day; camp No. 29 on Colorado. Some of the boys went hunting and
Levi and Tom S. attacked two or three old buffalo and got the worst of
the fight, as they were badly scared and run like good fellows. Weather
very fine.

Mar. 30th.   This morning we took the old road again for Chadburn,
but after traveling it for ten miles we lost it, so concluded to take our course
straight for home. We have seen plenty of buffalo to-day. Sharp Pistol
Tom killed one. About 3 o'clock we stopped and ate dinner. Buffalo are
plentiful here, George and Caesar nailed a yearling, Caesar held it while
George shot it. They have eaten the grass off very short so we concluded
to travel on till we found better grass, but soon found burnt prairie where
there was none at all. We rode on till 9 o'clock where we found a little, we
hoppled our horses and lay down in the open prairie for camp No. 29;
weather pleasant.

Mar. 31st.   We found a cold norther blowing this morning. We saddled
and started without any breakfast, expecting to find water in Jim Ned but
we crossed the head of it at noon and didn't get a drop. We then came to
a range of mountains, and after traveling till three o'clock P.M. we concluded to stop and broil some beef without water. After eating a hasty
meal we started on and in a few moments came to plenty of water. Here
we struck camp No. 30, and ate another hearty meal without bread. Sharp
Pistol Tom went hunting and found a ranch. He came back to camp and
took Sam to visit the ranch. They found the door open but no one there.
Pillows and clothes were scattered around the house, as though the Indians
had robbed the house. They found some flour, meat, tallow and coffee, and
took a little of each. Then we ate still heartier of bread, meat and coffee,
and went to bed; we think we are on Pecan Bayou.

April 1st.   To-day makes two months since we left home, expecting to
be back in one. They may be uneasy about us at home but we are all right

side up with care yet. After eating an old-fashioned breakfast, that is, both meat and bread, we took a northeast course for home. We soon got off the mountains and crossed the Bayou. Then we got into a black jack thicket, and saw a few deer, Sam was lucky enough to break ones thigh and our dog caught it. After getting through the thicket we came to the head of Deep Creek, and rode down a few miles where we found some small pools of rain water, and ate dinner. We made our fire in the bed of the creek which was a solid rock. After we had got to cooking nicely we were surprised by a noise like the blasting of rock, and fire and ashes flew in all directions. The Col. was badly scared and said he believed someone shot at him. But it was only the rock beneath the fire that burst. We continued to cook on the fire, but soon there came another blast louder, clearer, deadlier than before, like the bursting of a volcano. It covered our victuals in ashes, scattered fire and hot rocks over our saddles, blankets, and clothes for several feet around. That satisfied us, we moved our cooking up on the bank and finished eating in peace. After resting awhile we started on and rode till dark and found no water. Some of the boys thought we were close to Uncle George Greer's Ranch on Hubbard Creek, and we soon heard the barking of dogs, but it was Bob Sloan's Ranch on Deep Creek. We rode up to the house and borrowed some bacon from Mr. Brewer and got directions to a camping place not far off, where we struck camp No. 31. Mr. B. went to camp with us and stayed till bed time and talked about all things in general and nothing in particular.

April 2nd.   This morning Sam offered Mrs. Brewer an old tin cup to pay for the one she loaned us, which had got broken but she did not accept. She told us some surprising news, to-wit: the marriage of Mrs. Sloan, and Miss Catherine Greer. George and Tom S. got separated from us to-day and did not get with us any more. A little below the forks of Hubbard we met Joe Matthews and Gen. Miller and ate dinner with them. They told us news both good and bad. We were glad to hear of several newcomers into the world in our neighborhood and astonished to hear of so many marriages, but were very sorry to hear of the death of Mr. McKelvey and Miss Schoolcraft. After dark we rode out in the hills and laid down in camp No. 32. We miss Bill's long yarns very much as they were interesting and sometimes quite diverting.

April 3rd.   About sunrise we were on our horses aiming to get home to-day. There was a very hard sand storm blowing from the Plains so thick we could not see much over a hundred yards around. We stopped at Hoover's Ranch and got breakfast, and then rolled on. We bid Sharp

Pistol Tom adieu; he went down Hubbard, and we turned across the ridge to Clear Fork. About noon we found ourselves right-side-up at home, and in about two hours the other boys came in; they stayed at Lynch's last night.

Thus ends a journey in which we have all suffered fatigue and hunger alike, and gone through wet and dry, cold and hot together. In all probability the same party will never be out together again, so uncertain are the events of life.

*Shackelford County Courthouse
Albany, Texas — built in 1883.*

The Index

The Index, which was not provided in the original 1936 edition, was prepared by Miss Alice Reynolds of Albany, Texas.

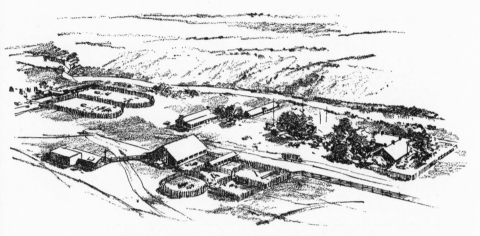

Lambshead — Headquarters Matthews Ranch since 1900.

The Reynolds Family

BENJAMIN FRANKLIN
REYNOLDS (1)   *m.*   SALLIE BARBER   ARCHIBALD CAMPBELL   *m.*   MARY GRAHA

several children including: *several children including:*

BARBER WATKINS REYNOLDS   *m.*   ANNE MARIA CAMPBELL

JOHN ARCHIBALD REYNOLDS (died in childhood)

[1867]   GEORGE THOMAS REYNOLDS   *m.*   LUCINDA ELIZABETH MATTHEWS

[1879]   WILLIAM DAVID REYNOLDS   *m.*   { MARY BYRD
{ SUSAN ALICE MATTHEWS *

SUSAN EMILY REYNOLDS   *m.*   { SAMUEL PIERCE NEWCOMB
{ NATHAN LOOMIS BARTHOLOMEW

GLENN REYNOLDS   *m.*   AUGUSTA LEMONT RUSSELL

[1879]   BENJAMIN FRANKLIN REYNOLDS (2)   *m.*   FLORENCE REBECCA MATTHEW

[1883]   PHINEAS WATKINS REYNOLDS   *m.*   ROSEANNAH MARION MATTHEWS

[1876]   SALLIE ANN REYNOLDS   *m.*   JOHN ALEXANDER MATTHEWS

The condensed charts show how the Reynolds and Matthews families were woven together by marriages.

* *The couples that linked the two families are indicated by dates of the marriages printed in green.*

KEY TO BRANDS SHOWN ON FRONT COVER

JOS	8	M O	∧<	✕
	Spanish Gourd	M O	A V	*Long X*
JOSEPH BECK MATTHEWS	BARBER WATKINS REYNOLDS	REYNOLDS & MATTHEWS *formerly J. A. Matthews*	J. A. MATTHEWS *Lambshead*	REYNOLDS CATTLE CO.

Most members of both families had their individual brands: Ben F. Reynolds used YL connected; George T. Reynolds a KEYSTONE; *W. D. Reynolds,* THREE LINKS; *P. W. Reynolds branded Z; N. L. Bartholomew, —11— (bar eleven bar) F. E. Conrad branded FE; M. V. Hoover, UNO; Sam P. Newcomb, V and Glenn Reynolds used the AV in Arizona.*